Caravans to Oblivion

Caravans to Oblivion

The Armenian Genocide, 1915

G. S. Graber

Foreword by Roger W. Smith, Ph.D.
Professor of Government, College of William and Mary
Council Member, Institute on the Holocaust and Genocide

John Wiley & Sons, Inc.

New York • Chichester • Brisbane • Toronto • Singapore

Library of Congress Cataloging-in-Publication Data:

Graber, G. S.
    Caravans to oblivion: the Armenian genocide, 1915 / G.S.
Graber.
        p.   cm.
    Includes bibliographical references (p.   ) and index.
    ISBN 0-471-11975-X (alk. paper)
    1. Armenian massacres, 1915–1923.   I. Title.
DS195.5.G72 1996
956.6'200491992—dc20
                                                                96-4355

Printed in the United States of America

10 9 8 7 6 5 4 3 2 1

For Beverly

CONTENTS

FOREWORD

Genocide has occurred in all periods of human history, but it has been especially prominent in the twentieth century. This century, in many ways a century of reason and progress, has also been an age of genocide, in which political regimes, in the name of history, biology, and nationalism, have claimed the lives of more than 60 million persons. Although the defeat of Nazi Germany brought with it the cry "Never again," genocide has been committed numerous times since then in Asia, Africa, Latin America, and Europe. In fact, since 1945, genocide has claimed the lives of more persons than all the civil and international wars combined during the same period.

Despite the evidence of so much politically inspired killing, with Bosnia and Rwanda the latest examples, many of us still tend to think of genocide as the province of the bestial, mad, or primitive. Genocide, however, is a human crime, one that animals are not capable of performing; it requires sustained organization, rationalization, and the cover-up known as denial of genocide. If the ends of genocide are often mad or at least irrational, the means chosen are carefully calculated; perpetrators wait for the "right" moment to carry out the destruction. As for being primitive, genocides do occur among such societies, but they are also committed by perpetrators like the

Nazis and the Bosnian Serbs, who have belonged to high civilizations. In fact, all of these labels are ways of evading a recognition that ordinary human beings have a capacity for destroying their fellows when caught up in certain political and social conditions. By speaking of the bestial, mad, and primitive, we minimize awareness of how often genocide has taken place in the twentieth century, and we also prevent understanding of why and how genocide takes place.

A second tendency is to relegate genocide to the past. Somehow, we seem to think that because we cried "Never again," genocide cannot occur in the present or the future. A corollary is that past genocides should simply be forgotten; they are over with, we cannot change the outcome, and they have no relevance to the present. But genocide is occurring, and there are many signs that, unless we take steps now, it will continue, perhaps even increase, in the twenty-first century. In fact, past genocides, and especially the Armenian Genocide, point to significant links between past, present, and future.

Remembrance of past genocides is important for at least four reasons. First, through remembrance we show respect and compassion for the victims and, in so doing, give evidence of our own humanity. Second, genocides that are committed, denied, and then forgotten send a clear signal to would-be perpetrators that they can slaughter a whole people and get away with it. Hitler knew this well as he laid plans for total war and the extermination of Jews and others: "Who, after all, speaks today of the annihilation of the Armenians?" Third, if we begin by dismissing genocides from the recent past, there will be no sense of urgency about preventing genocide in the present or future. Genocide will seem a rare occurrence, rather than an ongoing threat to overcome. Fourth, past cases of genocide may provide knowledge about why genocides take place and lead to an early warning system that could help prevent future atrocities from occurring.

The Armenian Genocide of 1915-1917, which claimed more than a million lives, is instructive with regard to all of these issues, but especially in relation to the question of understanding and prevention. Indeed, there is now a consensus among scholars that the Armenian genocide, which was the first large-scale genocide in the twentieth century, is the prototype of much of the genocide that has occurred since 1945. Some of the patterns found in the Armenian case have appeared again and again: There is a divided (or plural) society in which one ethnic group strives to dominate other distinct groups. This can lead to a quest for autonomy, even separation, and the challenge, real or imagined, to the control of government by the ruling ethnic group. Such demands are likely to be made at a time of political crisis, whether due to internal or external causes, and in the process there is often an increasing emphasis on nationalism. If civil or international war breaks out, the likelihood of genocide is greatly enhanced; genocide can now proceed under the cover of war, and the victims can be blamed for their own destruction. All of this is followed by denial of the genocide, international bodies speak briefly about war crime, and after a short period, the world forgets about the events.

There are, however, many different means that can be used to eliminate an ethnic group. In Rwanda, 800,000 persons were killed in a space of two months by a technology consisting of machetes and clubs. In Bosnia, it was a combination of artillery, rifles, concentration camps, and mass rape. Armenians were destroyed in still other ways: The leaders were rounded up on April 24, 1915 (now commemorated as Martyrs' Day), imprisoned briefly, then executed; the younger men were conscripted into the army, disarmed, used as pack animals, and then killed in small groups. Then it was the turn of the women, children, and old persons, who could not possibly have constituted any military threat to the Young Turk government: They were deported into the Syrian Desert, where they died from exposure, starvation, and direct killing.

The distinctive feature of the Armenian genocide, which sets it apart from the post-1945 examples to which it is otherwise related, is deportation. Henry Morgenthau, the American ambassador to the Ottoman Empire, recognized as early as June 1915 that the deportations "represented a new method of massacre. When the Turkish authorities gave the orders for these deportations, they were merely giving the death warrant to a whole race; they understood this well, and, in their conversations with me, they made no particular attempt to conceal the fact." Morgenthau goes on to add that from April to October 1915, the caravans of death could be seen "winding in and out of every valley and climbing up the sides of nearly every mountain—moving on and on, [those deported] scarcely knew whither, except that every road led to death."

In describing the caravans of death, Morgenthau exposes genocide for the radical evil it is, and he gives us new reasons for remembering the Armenian genocide, the forgotten genocide:

> In a few days, what had been a procession of normal human beings became a stumbling horde of dust-covered skeletons, ravenously looking for scraps of food, eating any offal that came their way, crazed by the hideous sights that filled every hour of their existence, sick with all the diseases that accompany such hardships and privations, but still prodded on and on by the whips and clubs and bayonets of their executioners.
>
> And thus, as the exiles moved, they left behind them another caravan—that of dead and unburied bodies, of old

men and women dying in the last stages of typhus, dysentery, and cholera, of little children lying on their backs and setting up their last piteous wails for food and water. There were women who held up their babies to strangers, begging them to take them and save them from their tormentors.

Finally, it should be noted that the Turkish government has denied for more than eighty years that the genocide even took place. Given such intransigence, healing and closure can take place only by the world recognizing and acknowledging the historical reality of the Armenian genocide.

> Roger W. Smith
> Professor of Government
> College of William and Mary

INTRODUCTION

Until fairly recently, the attempt by the Young Turks to eliminate the Armenian minority in the Ottoman Empire was referred to as the forgotten genocide. This was due in no small part to the denial, ever since modern Turkey was born under Kemal Atatürk (then Mustafa Kemal) in 1923, of any centrally organized and executed program of annihilation.

But this slaughter is no longer forgotten. While the genocide against the Armenians has not received anything like the breadth of analysis given to the holocaust unleashed by the Nazis on European Jews, there is now a wealth of commentary backed up by original sources. There is enough source material, released over the past few years by various government sources, to satisfy the greatest of skeptics. This source material consists of authenticated copies of actual telegrams sent from the Young Turks' Ministry of the Interior, together with affidavits and testimonies gathered when it was believed that Britain and France would actually honor their pledge to bring the guilty to trial. That they did not is one of the aspects of the story told in this book.

In addition to source material, there is now a great deal of first-rate scholarship in which objective analysis reveals the story of predator and prey in the first genocide of our century. Studies by Richard Hovannisian and Vahjakn Dadrian, for example (listed in the section on suggested reading), provide admirable commentary for anyone who seeks to come to grips with the subject.

For the lay reader, embarking on a history that begins in 1913 in the Ottoman Empire is rather like being cast adrift in a rudderless boat. The Ottoman Empire at the time was far removed from anything for which a Western experience provides some anchor. It has often been described as backward, or more famously as the Sick Man of Europe. Despite the attempt by the Young Turk leaders to introduce modernism, the Ottoman Empire was, to any visitor, perplexing, remote, and impossible to classify. For this reason I have opted to introduce the reader to this empire through the eyes of a German army officer. Although I suspect that neither the reader nor I would have much in common with the crusty, unbending, and somewhat limited General Otto Liman von Sanders, his reactions to what he saw when he first took up his appointment as leader of the German military mission to the Ottomans were probably those that most of us, reared in the West, would have had. He serves well, I believe, as an introduction to the world of scheming, frenetic, and alarming jockeying for position in which he found himself immersed.

There are other complications for the reader. One of these is the geographical location of the Armenians. They had occupied the eastern region of Anatolia, or Asia Minor, many centuries before the Turks arrived as conquerors. Most maps designate this region as historic Armenia. The area on the eastern Mediterranean known as Cilicia, or Little Armenia, had also been home to the Armenians since before the Crusades. On the eve of the First World War, some two million Armenians lived in these parts of the Ottoman Empire. But even

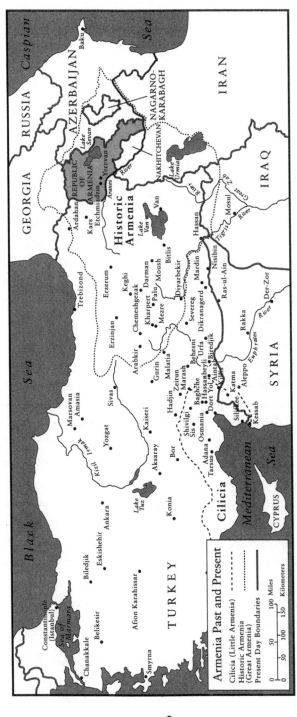

Reprinted with permission of the Regents of the University of California, from: *Survivors: An Oral History of the Armenian Genocide*, by Donald E. Miller and Lorna Touryan Miller, 1993.

3

more relevant to the political aspects of this story is the fact that another two million lived in tsarist Russia. Armenians therefore bestrode a frontier between Ottomans and Russians, a frontier continuously under dispute. From the start of the nineteenth century, the tsars had seen it as their duty to expand across the Caucasus to defend the Christian minorities there; the Ottomans had seen this as thinly veiled imperialism.

The Armenians have a complex history. They were situated in Anatolia before a series of foreign invaders (the Turks were the last in a long line) made them subject to one overlord after another. The Armenians thus became pawns of history. Their fate was determined by the machinations of foreign powers anxious to install themselves within the decaying Ottoman Empire for strategic or economic reasons. What the Armenians expected and desired became buried in issues the foreign powers considered far more important: the pursuit of political gain or the notion of *raison d'état*. Therefore, much of our story takes place in the embassies of the powers in Constantinople, where the professional diplomats of the age attempted to pursue their country's advantage at the Sublime Porte, as the seat of the Ottoman government was then known. These diplomats were often energetic and resourceful. It is difficult, for example, not to have a grudging respect for Baron Hans von Wangenheim, the German ambassador, who despite his attempt to distance himself from what was happening to the Armenians, at least seemed to have a better concept than most as to what made the Young Turk leaders tick. It is equally difficult to respect Gerald Fitzmaurice, the expert, or dragoman, at the British embassy, whose judgments were so often wide of the mark.

The political vehicle of the Young Turks, who ran the empire while the genocide took place, was their party, the Committee of Union and Progress (CUP). Its name in Turkish is *Ittihad ve Teraki*. The Young Turks were also called Unionists or *Ittihadists*.

Turkey still does not believe in an open society. Only in a limited and halting fashion has source material about this period been translated from the Turkish into the European languages. When such material is available, it is normally accompanied by an editorial that reconfirms the Turkish view: Armenians were radicals bent on allying themselves with Russia. I have also obtained source material in German or French, which I have translated myself.

The vast number of Armenians who were slaughtered in the genocide had nothing whatever to do with politics; ironically, most victims of this and other genocides were people who never had a political idea in their lives. Why then should historians or politicians with an ax to grind make political figures out of them? For me, the abiding picture of the Armenian genocide is the Armenian caravans. Out in the desert, probably in transit to some arid final destination in Mesopotamia, women and children carried their pathetic bundles to their death through exposure or disease. Alongside them at intervals marched the paramilitary troops, whose license included the right to rob, slaughter, and leave for dead. Where were the Armenian men? They had already been roped together and shot, their corpses rotting around the countryside, much to the displeasure of Grand Vizier Talaat at the Ministry of the Interior. (He had specifically instructed the murderers to bury the corpses.) Most of these victims had never expressed a political slogan in their lives. But because of political decisions reached elsewhere, the Armenians were starved, mutilated, or simply left to expire under the unremitting sun. This is the picture we should keep in mind, especially when our narrative shows politicians exchanging views about what is politically appropriate.

There is another important aspect of the genocide. Throughout the three generations in Turkey since the events described in this book, the Turkish establishment has denied that the massacre ever occurred in such a form as to warrant the use of the term *genocide*. Officially, Turkey has maintained that the massacre lacks the chief prerequisite of any genocide—it must be centrally organized and administered.

If it was not genocide, what was it in the official Turkish view? It was a series of events, uncoordinated and sporadic, that took place in the heightened conditions of war and resulted from the fury of sections of the Turkish populace at the machinations of the Armenians. What were these machinations? They consisted in the main of large-scale defections to the other side, to Russia.

This Turkish posture has produced nothing but scorn among Armenians, who say it is a cover-up for the Young Turk policy of systematic annihilation of the Armenian community.

These two totally opposing and mutually exclusive views have produced the polarity that has characterized historical assessment of these events and has contributed to the deep well of acrimony and bitterness that permeates the subject.

Is it possible to tell the story without landing too heavily in one camp? I have attempted to do so, but I do have a viewpoint based on such study of the material as I have undertaken, and perhaps I should announce it now. I do believe there was a genocide; I believe this can be proven from the documents. But I also believe that had I been an Armenian in Turkey at the time, I, too, given the enormity of the provocation my community had sustained, would have crossed the military line and joined the Russians. What is more, I do not believe that this admission weakens the cause of the Armenians. For what possible role could have been played in these so-called defections by women, children, the infirm, and the elderly?

Autocratic governments (and certainly during the First World War, the Young Turk regime was autocratic) like nothing better than to stage bloody attacks on defenseless sections of their populations and then claim that these events took place because of the justified rage of their patriotic citizens. We know, for example, that the staging of Kristallnacht (the night during which the Nazis arranged their national attack against Jews and Jewish property in November 1938) was centrally co-ordinated via Reinhard Heydrich's teleprinter at Gestapo headquarters in Berlin and had nothing to do with spontaneous expressions of rage among the German populace— despite the enlistment of the Nazi propaganda machine in this analysis. And we know, and shall in the course of this study illustrate, that in 1915 the Young Turk genocide was masterminded via the teleprinter by Talaat at the Ministry of the Interior at Constantinople.

It is not the purpose of this study to provide a cultural history of the Armenians. The reader interested in familiarizing him or herself with Armenian achievement will find several titles suggested in the section "Recommended Further Reading."

Chapter 1

A General Arrives

As the train approached Constantinople on the fourteenth of December, 1913, General of Cavalry Otto Liman von Sanders checked his own appearance and then, well aware of the importance of first impressions, made one final inspection of the German officers accompanying him. These consisted of captains or majors, all specialists in some branch of military endeavor and now resplendent in their dress uniforms. Liman von Sanders was the oldest and most senior among them. He was approaching his fifty-ninth birthday, having spent no fewer than thirty-nine of his years in the Prussian army. Although in the recent past he had held a number of senior appointments, this was the first time his role was to land him in the limelight.

Some six months earlier, while commanding officer of the 22nd Division at Cassel, Liman had received a flattering summons from the German military cabinet inviting him to head up a mission to help the Ottoman Turks reorganize and modernize their army.

It was not the first time that Prussia had responded to a request from the Sublime Porte to send a team of officers to help modernize the Turkish army. At various intervals throughout the nineteenth century, there had been a German military presence at Constantinople. What was different about this delegation was its size. There were no fewer than forty officers in the party.

From a longer historical perspective, it was a complete reversal for the Ottomans to have the need to invite military representatives from a foreign country to reform their army. In their successive campaigns to conquer Europe during their heyday of military prowess in the fourteenth and fifteenth centuries, no European armies had been able to withstand the Turkish cavalry or infantry. Not until the Turks stood at the gates of Vienna in 1529 was their drive into Europe halted. From this time forward, Turkish military might declined; the Ottoman Empire disintegrated, and successive Ottoman regimes were constantly on the verge of bankruptcy, tottering from one calamity to another until rescued by foreign aid. Now, compelled as they were to turn to the hated foreigner to learn the modern skills essential to their survival, the Turks were selective in their choice of whom to approach for advice and which institutions they might copy.

Given these circumstances, the German emperor, William II, was determined to increase German influence in the Ottoman Empire. Germany had minor holdings on the African continent, but these were insufficient to appease William's appetite for imperial expansion, an activity to which Germany had arrived late in the day. He had visited Turkey in 1889 and again in 1898. On the latter visit he had appeared in Jerusalem, then part of the Ottoman Empire, dressed as a knight on a white charger. He bestowed gifts on those he wished to impress with

Germany's recently developed but huge industrial potential. He had dedicated himself for some time to the construction of the Berlin-to-Baghdad railway. This was the prime example of German ambition within the Ottoman Empire and of William's wish to make certain it was German capital that developed the backward empire. But there were ramifications. For example, to avoid antagonizing the unpredictable Sultan Abdülhamīd II, the emperor had refrained from joining the other European powers in their condemnation of this sultan's persecution of the Armenians in 1894–96. There had been a long tradition of animosity toward the Christian Armenians within the largely Muslim empire, which intensified during the 1890s when the Armenians attempted to improve their political and social lot. To systematize and coordinate the actions against the Armenians in the mid-1890s Abdülhamīd had formed his battalions of Hamideye troops (which he named after himself), whose task was to decimate the occupants of Armenian villages and replace them with Muslims.

There is little doubt that Liman von Sanders, though no historian, had familiarized himself with the political developments at Constantinople since the mid-1890s. Winds of change had begun to course through Abdülhamīd's empire in the last years of the nineteenth century. The sultan sensed these winds, but their effect was compounded by his paranoia. He saw himself surrounded by enemies bent on unseating him. He had not been blind to the value of Western education and scientific inquiry—it was Abdülhamīd who had founded the very few institutions of higher learning in the empire—but he sensed that the intellectual disciplines being taught there could produce the kind of independence of thought and action that might bring about his downfall. In this he was correct. The younger generation, particularly the graduates from the military colleges, were certain that the Ottomans must rescue themselves from the crippling and stifling atmosphere of the Abdülhamīd regime if the empire were to survive and have any chance of prospering.

In 1908 a new political party named *Ittihad ve Teraki* (Committee of Union and Progress), led mainly by dynamic young army officers, forced the sultan to establish a constitution to guarantee basic liberties. (This same constitution had been voided by Abdülhamīd some thirty years earlier on the grounds that its implementation would cause revolution.) Within a year of the reintroduction of the Constitution, Abdülhamīd assembled all the forces within the empire most likely to undermine the constitution. In 1909 these forces made a bid for the return of the old regime. They were suppressed, however, and Abdülhamīd was forced to give up his throne. From that day forward, the fortunes of the Ottoman Empire rested in the hands of the Young Turks, who, under the banner of the *Ittihad ve Teraki,* gradually assumed control of the empire. Succeeding sultans became basically titular in importance. (Chapter 3 will take a much closer look at these events.)

In a meeting shortly before Liman's departure for the Middle East, William II had made a special point of instructing him how to behave in any delicate political situation. He told Liman, "It must be entirely immaterial to you whether the Young Turks are in power or the Old Turks. You are concerned with the army alone. Drive politics out of the corps of Turkish officers. Its greatest defect is its political activity."[1]

This sentiment ignored the fact that the appearance of a large German military mission at the center of the Ottoman Empire was almost certain to cause a frisson in diplomatic circles. It is possible the emperor believed that the bluff and burly German ambassador to the Sublime Porte, Baron von

Baron von Wangenheim, German ambassador to the Sublime Porte. Astute and hardworking, he had a sophisticated appreciation of the personalities of the Young Turk leaders. (Bildarchiv Preussischer Kulturbesitz)

Wangenheim, could manage such political maneuvering as was necessary to increase German influence among the Ottomans. Wangenheim was a man of considerable diplomatic experience; before taking the embassy at Constantinople, he had seen service at Saint Petersburg, Copenhagen, Madrid, Athens, and Mexico City. He also had at the embassy an experienced military attaché named Major von Stempel. It was thus fair to believe that Liman might be able to restrict himself to the reform of the Ottoman army.

It was Wangenheim, in any event, who had added a note to the original request made from Constantinople for a German military mission. "The appointee," he wrote in requesting a high-ranking officer to head the mission, "must be a person of eminent military ability and one of wide experience in the work of the general staff. Furthermore, he should be a strong character who knows how to gain his point . . . . In case of refusal, it is to be feared that the Sublime Porte may turn to other powers, since it is determined to break with the present, insufficient system of military reform."[2] Evidently, Wangenheim was aware that the rulers of Turkey did not consider themselves bound to any one of the countries anxious to install themselves within the Ottoman Empire for economic and military gain, and the Turks would not hesitate to play one applicant against another to their own advantage. There had been, for example, an English naval mission in Constantinople for some years under the leadership of Admiral Arthur H. Limpus, whose function was to assist in the buildup of an Ottoman navy. It was clear that if Germany did not provide assistance, one of the other European powers would be only too happy to do so.

In Liman, Wangenheim certainly got what he wanted: a strong character, but one who, Wangenheim was soon to realize, was constitutionally unable to bend with the wind and had never heard the word *compromise*.

As the train pulled in to the station at Sirkedji on the first day of his tour of duty, Liman and his fellow officers heard a crash of military music. Liman was the first to reach the receiving line and was delighted to see the minister of war, Izzet

Pasha, whom he had met in Germany and whom he knew spoke some German. It was also apparent that the delegation was not being met by any representative from the German embassy. Wangenheim was not there; neither was the military attaché. Rather than take offense at what might have been considered a slight, Liman was philosophical—perhaps the ambassador was attempting to minimize the importance of the occasion so as to avoid any critical comment in the foreign press.

Liman was given offices at the Ottoman War Ministry. About three weeks after his arrival, he was told that Izzet Pasha was too ill to come to work. It was only fitting that Liman pay his respects to the invalid, and so he did—but during his visit he was appalled to learn that Izzet had been forced to resign in a coup d'état led by Enver Pasha on January 13, 1914. (Enver and Izzet were not related; *pasha* was an honorary title placed after a name to indicate a high rank or office in Turkey. Similarly, the title *bey* was used as a courtesy.) Such coups were staged on a regular basis to reform the army. Liman had neither the taste nor the temperament for such sudden changes. At his office the next day, he was further dismayed by an unannounced visit from Enver Pasha, who was now wearing a general's uniform and claimed to be the new minister of war. Liman had previously met Enver at the Ottoman embassy in Berlin where, some two years before, he had held the rank of major.

Enver was a short, very slim young man, at the time only thirty-two years old. (The incumbent sultan, the successor to Abdülhamīd, shook his head upon learning of Enver's appointment and said that Enver was far too young.) A 1902 graduate of the staff college, Enver had his first army appointment as a captain posted to the 3rd Army in Macedonia, where for three years he conducted operations against the Macedonian guerrillas. The 3rd Army in Macedonia was well known in

Constantinople as a hotbed of political dissidence. When in 1906 he was promoted to major, Enver had joined the nucleus of conspirators in the Young Turk movement. In the elaborate police state formed by Abdülhamīd, teams of agents were sent to collect evidence against those, chiefly junior officers, who were bent on introducing constitutional government in the empire. Consequently, Enver disappeared into the hills to avoid unwelcome questions, but he reappeared on July 24, 1908, as one of the leaders of the Young Turk revolution, dedicated to the introduction of parliamentary government and to the modernization of many aspects of Ottoman life.

Enver's experience at the Ottoman embassy in Berlin, where he was assigned after the revolution, had confirmed in him a lifelong admiration for the German military. He even sported a Prussian military mustache, thin and upward curling, which some unkind Western observers maintained gave him the appearance of a tailor's dummy. Nevertheless, Enver's effect on the Turkish populace was electric. Of the three men who formed the triumvirate that took control of and then led the Ottoman Empire until the end of the First World War, Enver undoubtedly had the most personal charisma. He had a profound sense of personal mission, courted danger with no regard for his own safety, and tended to appear wherever the action was. In 1911 he resigned his post in Berlin to volunteer for service in the Libyan war, in which he fought with distinction. On June 5, 1912, he received a promotion to lieutenant colonel and, returning to Constantinople the same year, used his considerable power within the Committee of Union and Progress to ensure that his friend, Talaat, received the important post of secretary-general.

None of these attributes, including the heroic stance Enver adopted, engaged the support of Liman von Sanders. In the first place, Enver's behavior placed him in a radical camp, and Liman did not like radicals. Even worse, Liman disagreed with virtually every strategic decision Enver reached in the succeeding years. In his view, Enver's decisions were seldom based on sound and proven military considerations. During five years of tenuous collaboration, the two men moved unfailingly from one disagreement to another. One historian has suggested that there was bound to be some disharmony between them from the outset because Liman, who always stuck unreservedly to his guns in an argument, was somewhat deaf, and actually used his deafness as a weapon.[3] In addition, Enver's German was not as good as he pretended, and he often missed the point of what Liman was saying. A man like Enver, whose actions were governed by a deep sense of personal mission and who kept inspirational pictures of Napoléon and Frederick the Great above his desk, was unlikely to admit any deficiency in linguistic ability, lest this give his opponent an edge in argument or reveal some fallibility that might put him at a disadvantage.

It was not long before the sparks began to fly. As newly appointed minister of war, Enver initiated his rule by dismissing one thousand officers of the Ottoman army. Liman was outraged. Under the terms of his appointment, he was supposed to be consulted on the question of replacements, especially the replacements of those of higher rank. Furthermore, it was no secret that a number of the discharged officers were being held under arrest in the office just below the one in which Liman was sitting. He was dead set on disassociating himself (and, of course, Germany) from this action, which to him appeared indiscriminate. Not only had he not been consulted, but he worried that he might be held accountable.

Liman's deteriorating relations with Enver were not the only problem he faced. Within the German community in

Constantinople, Liman rapidly earned the reputation of being impossible. Liman's view was that he had been appointed by the emperor, and this gave him ambassadorial rank. When invited to some special gathering for dinner, for example, he was very aware of where he was seated and would take umbrage if he was not placed near the head of the table. But such resentments were inconsequential compared with the state of almost continuous war that existed between Liman and Ambassador von Wangenheim. The relationship was so bad that within a few months of the outbreak of the First World War, Wangenheim called his boss, Arthur Zimmermann, secretary of state at the German foreign office, and complained, "Liman has completely severed his personal relations with me and persecutes the entire staff of the Embassy with incredible chicanery."[4]

Not blind to the impression he was making on his peers in Constantinople, Liman began to send urgent messages to the military cabinet in Germany, asking for a new posting. For reasons that are difficult to determine even today, his request was refused. Liman began to threaten resignation; he repeatedly asked the military cabinet for a new posting. Both the military cabinet and the foreign office would delay a week before replying, in the hope that the crusty Liman would relent—and learn to control his temper. Invariably, William would cable him to announce that he was still needed at Constantinople.

Liman had ample reason for wanting to leave. Within a few weeks of his arrival, it became clear to him that to arrange any modernization in this chaotic and reactionary empire was a herculean task. He quickly learned that things were different in Turkey.

The first overwhelming evidence of this came at an inspection visit he made to Tshorlu. "I had inspected troops of the 8th Division," he wrote, which I found in the most wretched condition. The officers had not received pay in six to eight months and they and their families were compelled to get their subsistence from the troop messes. The men had not seen pay for years, were undernourished and dressed in ragged uniforms. Of the company sent to the railway station as a guard of honor, a considerable part wore torn boots or shoes, others were barefooted. The division commander explained that he could not hold large exercises because the men were too weak and could not march with such defective footgear. I informed Enver in writing of my finding and requested remedial action, whereupon Enver dismissed the division commander, Colonel Ali Risa Bey. On learning this, I went to Enver and informed him that any military activity on my part in Turkey was impossible if those officers were dismissed who told me the truth.[5]

Enver must have wondered at the naiveté of the leader of the German military mission. Did Liman not realize that the Turkish army had a small supply of uniforms and boots in reasonable condition, which was rushed from one parade to another as dictated by necessity? Was Liman truly that ignorant of the state of affairs in the land that one tsar had labeled the Sick Man of Europe only fifty years earlier?

Chapter 2

TURKS AND ARMENIANS

In the latter half of the nineteenth century and in a gathering chorus, public officials and scholars with far greater vision than Liman von Sanders had expressed reservations about what was happening in the Ottoman Empire. German Chancellor Otto von Bismarck had commented that the entire Eastern Question (the term used in the West to describe the controversies surrounding the future of the Ottomans) was not worth the bones of one Pomeranian grenadier. In an 1853 conversation with the British ambassador at Saint Petersburg, Russian Tsar Nicholas I said of the Ottoman Empire, "We have a sick man on our hands—a man gravely ill." A most damning assessment of the Ottomans was made by Oxford scholar J. A. R. Marriott, who in his 1919 *The Eastern Question* wrote, "The primary and most essential factor in the situation is the presence, embedded in the living flesh of Europe, of an alien substance. That substance is the Ottoman Turk. Akin to the European family neither in creed, in race, in language, in social customs, nor in political aptitudes and traditions, the Ottomans have for more than five hundred years presented to the European powers a problem, now tragic, now comic, now bordering almost on burlesque, but always baffling and paradoxical."[1]

Thus did most of the West perceive the Ottomans. But the object of this scorn, the Ottomans themselves, considered the West to be riddled with hypocrisy. From the Ottoman viewpoint, this hypocrisy was evident in the interest the West occasionally took in the fate of the Christian minorities of the empire. It was clear to the Ottomans, for instance, that repeated claims by a succession of Russian tsars that they had a special responsibility to protect the Christians of Anatolia and elsewhere were simply a rationalization of Russia's true purpose: to gain access to the Mediterranean and secure a foothold at Constantinople.

Among the Christians in need of protection, the ones whose name was most often on foreign lips were the Armenians. The Armenians had occupied their ancient homeland in the eastern areas of Anatolia for over twenty-five hundred years and had been a presence in Cilicia, on the northern Mediterranean, since the Crusades. The Ottoman Turks were relatively recent arrivals in this area, having been preceded by a host of other invaders: Greeks, Romans, Persians, Arabs and Byzantines. Thus the Armenian historical experience had been one of continuous occupation. The Armenians, however, had learned two things well. First, they had learned to preserve their cultural, linguistic, and religious identity; they were proud of the fact, for instance, that the Armenian nation had been the first to make Christianity its state religion. Second, they had managed to persuade a succession of conquerors that they were ideal citizens. One of the nineteenth-century Ottoman sultans even declared that the Armenians were his most loyal subjects, or, as he phrased it, his "most loyal *millet.*" (A *millet* is a national or religious group within the Ottoman Empire.)

The Ottoman Empire was a theocracy. In the great heyday of Ottoman conquest, it was understood that all minorities acquired by the empire would automatically be offered conversion to the true religion, Islam. However, there were those who, from the Ottoman point of view, were too obstinate, or possibly too stupid, to appreciate the superiority of Islam over all other creeds. These subjects were called *gaiour,* or "cattle." The Armenians adhered to their version of apostolic Christianity and preserved their language and traditions. That the Ottomans took the word *cattle* literally was frequently demonstrated over the centuries when, during periods of unrest, Armenian throats were slit in the same fashion as cattle might be slaughtered.

At the apex of the theocratic regime was the sultan, who also bore the title of *caliph,* meaning "successor to Muhammad." Among various temporal and spiritual duties, the caliph had to protect the canon law of Islam, called the *Sharia,* the revelation of the laws of God as articulated by the prophet Muhammad.

Historian Vahjakn Dadrian summarized the significance of the Sharia as follows: "The Sheriat [Sharia] comprised not only religious precepts, but a fixed and infallible doctrine of duties, including regulations of a political and juridical nature, whose prescriptions and proscriptions were restricted to the territorial jurisdiction of the State."[2]

As so-called cattle, the Armenians neither deserved nor were granted the liberties, political or legal, accorded to believers. Like the other minorities within the empire (Greek, Jews, and a host of other Christian sects), Armenians were second-class citizens. According to Dadrian, "The Koran specifically enjoined Mohammedans to fight against them . . . until they pay tribute by right of subjection, and they be reduced low. . . . The Sultan-Khalif's newly incorporated non-Muslim subjects were required to enter into a quasi-legal contract, the Akdi-Zimmet, whereby the ruler guaranteed the safeguard of their persons, their civil and religious liberties, and, conditionally, their properties, in exchange for the payment of poll and land taxes, and acquiescence to a set of social and legal disabilities."[3]

Another element in the Armenian condition played an increasingly important role as the nineteenth century advanced. As mentioned in the introduction, the lands of historic Armenia were divided between Russia and Turkey, two empires frequently at war with each other. There were about two million Armenians on each side of the frontier. Russia had repeatedly courted the Armenians of the Ottoman Empire, but these Armenians knew they would lose the individuality of their historic religion under the Russian steamroller. They would be coerced into becoming part of the Eastern Orthodox Church espoused by the tsars. They did not want to give up what they knew and treasured. Nonetheless, the Armenians realized that if Turkish aggression against them was to mount, the need to save their lives might overwhelm the question of religious choice. The Turks were all too conscious of the tsars' occasional courtship of the Ottoman Armenians, and they were intensely suspicious of it. Russia was, after all, their historic enemy across the Caucasus.

Unlike other minorities within the empire, however, the Armenians were without automatic external support. Other groups could always look abroad with some confidence for sponsorship or protection. It had become a traditional Russian ploy, for instance, to threaten reprisals against the Turks if they

persecuted the Bulgars or Serbs, who practiced Eastern Orthodox Christianity. For generations, tsars had promoted the concept of Moscow as the Third Rome and considered other
Orthodox Christians to be their responsibility. Likewise, the siz-
able and ancient Greek community in the Ottoman Empire
could count on support from Athens, and the smaller Catholic
communities were under the protection of France. The foreign
press might deal vociferously with what was happening to the
Armenians, but the Turks had come to view this as so much
empty noise. It was unbacked by the force of arms.

At the turn of the century, there were widespread mis-
conceptions about Armenians. It was a time when the percep-
tions of the English traveler were important because of the significance of Britain on the world stage. To these travelers,
generally titled young men of good background, Armenians
were *Levantine*, which to the British meant they were likely to
fleece anyone they could. "Even Jews have their good points,
but Armenians have none," wrote Sir Mark Sykes, revealing the
prejudices of the time.[4] Sir Mark evidently failed to see during
his travels that the Armenians did, in fact, constitute a nation
comprised of all economic and social categories. They were not
solely traders. A large Armenian peasantry garnering a living
from the soil had existed since time immemorial on the high
plateaus of eastern Anatolia. The very porters who carried Sir
Mark's bags at the Constantinople bazaars were more than
likely to have been Armenian, probably peasants transplanted
from rural farmlands under the policies of Abdülhamīd, who
was intent on getting rid of Armenians and replacing them
with Kurds and Circassians, good and reliable Muslims.

In the cities dwelt the Armenian *amiras,* the leading busi-
nesspeople who, some scholars claim, virtually dominated

Ottoman economic life. It has been suggested quite recently that by the end of the nineteenth century, 90 percent of internal trade and at least half of foreign trade was in Armenian hands.[5] In most cities of the empire, the overwhelming majority of lawyers, doctors, and skilled workers were Armenian. Before jumping mistakenly to the conclusion that this must inevitably have created a huge well of jealousy among the less fortunate Turks, remember that within the Turkish scheme of things, commerce remained a not-quite-acceptable activity for an adult male. A good Turk, it was thought, should go into government service or into a branch of the armed forces where, if he was really spectacular, he might attain the highest respect among the Ottomans by becoming a *gaza,* a warrior.

Just as visiting Conservatives from Britain tended to get the wrong picture of the Armenians, those other dedicated travelers from England, the Oxford aesthetes, drew a somewhat questionable picture of the Turkish peasant of Anatolia. "One is bound to like him if only for his courage and simplicity, and his blind fidelity and his loyalty"; so wrote one Oxford don who helped train a generation of British Arabists.[6] That this fidelity and loyalty could be mobilized occasionally in the inhuman work of destruction did not concern the travelers.

The rate of savage attacks on the Armenians increased radically in the last quarter of the nineteenth century, mostly in response to increased Armenian political activity. The reasons for this increased political activity are many, but one cause was that, of all the various communities within the empire, the Armenians were the best educated. It was the children of wealthy Armenians who finished their education in Paris or Geneva; it was the children of the Armenian middle classes who obtained their education at the foreign-administered missions in Anatolia. These missions were overwhelmingly American in origin and had been founded mainly in an attempt to seduce Muslims to Christianity. When this failed, the missions turned their efforts to the other Christian communities. They were only moderately successful in persuading Armenians to abandon the Armenian Church, but they did offer the opportunity to get an education and the Armenians took advantage of it. Given the general standard of illiteracy among the Turks, the Armenians became one of the best-educated groups in the empire. Another advantage of attending a mission school was that it often had a clinic staffed by nurses. This was a novelty in Anatolia, where there were few medical facilities available to Turks. When a Turk died, it was usually as a result of some epidemic of tuberculosis, dysentery, or malaria. As one scholar has pointed out, "Except in a very few cities there was simply no modern health care. The average Anatolian woman could expect to bear six children, of whom three would die before their fifth birthday."[7]

Minds that begin to inquire are eventually bound to ask political questions. Gradually, younger Armenians became aware of the liberties enjoyed in other parts of the world, and the passive role of bending one's head to Ottoman oppression became less and less tolerable. The Armenian Church, which had since olden times been the official mouthpiece of the community, became subject to criticism. A more radical approach was demanded, especially by the Armenian youth. Such radicalism in the Ottoman Empire was fueled by the Armenians of Russia, where for more than a generation the question of human rights had exercised all sections of the population and where the huge forces that were to culminate in the revolution of 1917 were in ferment.

The West occasionally attempted to persuade Sultan Abdülhamīd to deal more humanely with his Christian minorities. One of the provisions of the Treaty of Berlin (1878) compelled the sultan to introduce a constitution. Though he was finally persuaded to accept this, he abandoned the constitution shortly afterward on the grounds that its introduction would simply foster revolution. He had agreed to it temporarily only to silence the foreigners.

In consequence, all critics of the Abdülhamīd regime were driven abroad. It was in Geneva in 1887 that the first radical Armenian political organization was born. It was called *Hunchak,* meaning "bell," and it was revolutionary in its aims. It was followed in 1890 by the foundation of the much more important and longer-lived *Dashnakstutium.* Both organizations called for an independent Armenia. Their formation spelled the end of Armenian quietism; "The Armenian now demands, with gun in hand," claimed one slogan. "The Armenian was no longer prepared to wait for help from the Powers which would not materialize," one scholar has summarized. "He took the identity of his race into his own hand."[8]

This was basically a new position for the Armenians. Its effect on Abdülhamīd was predictable. He felt he was faced with a sinister revolution that he must use all his resources to combat.

When Armenian resistance first arose in 1893, however, it was not driven by urban radicals or intellectual leaders. Its voice was the Armenian peasantry in Sassun, deep in the Armenian mountains. It was not based primarily on a yearning for freedom; its cause was much nearer to the hearts of a peasant society. The wandering Kurdish tribes had been given tacit allowance by the sultan to extort the peasant Armenian communities in the way that gangsters extort protection money for use of their turf. According to historian Christopher J. Walker, "The Kurdish aghas [commanders] used to demand from them a kind of protection tax—an annual due of crops, cattle, silver, iron ore . . . agricultural implements or clothes. And when an Armenian girl married, her parents were forced to pass on to an agha half the sum which their son-in-law paid them as dowry. . . . In many places the Armenians were forced to pay double taxes."[9] It was well known in most of the foreign consulates throughout the empire that the Kurds had been assured by the authorities that they would never be called to account for these activities.[10]

By 1892 Abdülhamīd had authorized the formation of some thirty regiments of Hamideye, each about five hundred men strong and each composed of itinerant Kurds whose spoken or unspoken function was to suppress the Armenians. To defend themselves against the depredations of the Kurds and the corruption of the Turkish officials, Armenian peasants in the Sassun district retreated into the mountains and held out against successive attacks mounted by Kurds and regular Turkish army units. Despite the attempts of Armenian political activists to put an ideological slant on the resistance of the Armenian peasants, it is arguable that the peasants' fight had more to do with outrage at a system of double taxation than with a passionate belief in human liberty.

It would be wrong to assess the peasants' actions as purely defensive, however; they were a direct and organized challenge to Ottoman authority. And it would be equally wrong to assume that the intention of Abdülhamīd was simply to teach the insurgents a lesson. As he saw it, this kind of continuous harassment might lead to a withdrawal of the Armenians from their native villages—and their eventual replacement by Muslims. In the end, despite some early success, the Armenian peasants were overrun and murdered—men, women and children—in their mountain hideouts. The attempts of the Ottoman regime to conceal this indiscriminate massacre from the international press foundered on one circumstance: the British, under pressure from Liberal public opinion at home, had been compelled to increase their consular representation in the Armenian *vilayets* (provinces). Some perspicacious British consuls had seen what was happening and filed reports to the embassy at Constantinople, which in turn sent them to London. The press got wind of them, and soon the word *Sassun* became a rallying cry around which all those sympathizing with the Armenian predicament could gather.

The Armenian political leadership was well aware of this. It is difficult to see what the activists could do other than foster foreign support; clearly, no support was forthcoming from within the empire, and the Armenians were under daily attack. It was the foreigner, *faute de mieux,* to whom they had to turn.

It was the foreigner, after all, who repeatedly asked Abdülhamīd to ease the lot of his Christian minorities. It was the foreigner whom Abdülhamīd considered a disagreeable thorn in his side. The sultan became adept at making promises of reform to these insistent foreigners, and then never honoring any of them. "He seemed to be handing out reform and justice with his right hand," as one commentator has pithily put it, while "with his left he was dealing murder and atrocity on a scale hitherto unknown. In almost all impartial accounts there is mention of the complicity of soldiers, gendarmes and other officials."[11]

The killing was indeed "on a scale hitherto unknown." The murder and atrocity reached their peak from 1894 to

1896, when somewhere between 200,000 and 300,000 Armenians were slaughtered.

This became impossible to hide from the European powers or from tsarist Russia. The information gathered by consuls, especially British consuls, throughout this period gives a good idea of the climate of the age.

For example, the British consul at Trebizond, Consul Longworth, wrote to the British embassy at Constantinople on October 28, 1895: "I cannot offer my opinion as to other parts, but here at least, the Armenians were and are still in great stress: killed in cold blood, robbed of their goods, flung into gaol, not allowed to emigrate, blackmailed by the Moslems and persecuted by the authorities, the poor people are in the deepest despair. At Trebizond the troops were declared insufficient, but had they been more, their conduct was such that the carnage would have been greater."[12]

Longworth's reference to the insufficiency of the troops (who were supposedly there to maintain order) is a cynical commentary on the fact that the troops were as much to blame for the treatment of the Armenians as were the civilians. What Longworth had seen clearly had a considerable effect on him, because only four or five days later he wrote that the authorities persisted "in the make believe that there was an insurrectionary movement at Trebizond, unable though they are to name a single Turk as killed or wounded by Armenians on the occasion of the outbreak. Such dogged obduracy and perversity can only be possible in a shameless and despotic Government, supported by a people who had shown themselves to be murderers and robbers of the helpless and innocent."[13]

Other reports reached London, not necessarily penned by the personnel of the consulates. For example, a British cleric attached to an American mission, the Reverend Mr. Chambers, gave evidence of a massacre that took place at Akhisar. His report was sent to London on October 22, 1895:

As I entered the village of Akhisar on Sunday, a fearful stench greeted me. Several bodies that had that morning been removed from a well were being buried. I visited four wells, from one of them—ten minutes walk from the scene of the slaughter—fourteen bodies had been recovered, from another, two, from another, five. One had not yet been opened; there were bloodmarks on the stones covering it. In all, twenty three bodies have been recovered for burial. . . .

The murders were committed in the most inhuman manner: cudgels, knives, axes, swords and firearms were used. Young boys helped in the slaying. Ropes were tied to the feet of the dead and the bodies were dragged through the streets . . . and thrown into the wells. One old man of 75 years was tumbled in without being killed, and was left to die among the corpses of his friends.

There were almost 200 Armenian shops. . . . I was amazed to see what a clean sweep was made. The merchants' money, watches and other valuables were first secured, then the men killed and their account books, notes of hand and valuable papers, torn to shreds.

There were sixteen armed officials present . . . but their presence was evidently an encouragement to the killers. They could have stopped the slaughter at its inception or at any time during its course. . . . Instead of attempting to do so they acted as follows: the *Kol Aghassi* [a police officer] observed the killing for forty minutes and then taking with him three *zaptiehs* [police officers of another rank] rode to Gueve, five miles away, to give word to the *Kaimakam* [the commissioner of a subdistrict] who four hours after the slaughter commenced, arrived on the scene. This shows fiendish deliberation of movement. . . .

The killing of so many, the disposing of the bodies, the careful covering up of the wells, the washing of the blood-stains . . . all show a perfection of plan and deliberation of action impossible to an unprepared and suddenly aroused mob. . . . There has never been the slightest trace of Hunchagism [Armenian political activity] in Akhisar, the Armenians had no arms and made no resistance, nor did they do anything to bring on the affray.[14]

This report demonstrates that what happened at Akhisar was not the result of some spontaneous outburst of resentment against the Armenians, but the execution of a carefully and methodically planned slaughter. There was not even an Armenian political organization to lend some credence to the sultan's claim that he was dealing with terrorists. The massacre had become indiscriminate. All Armenians, regardless of gender or age, had become enemies of the state.

The concept that all Armenians were actual or potential terrorists was the facade for Abdülhamīd's actual intention to denude the Armenian *vilayets* of Armenians and replace them with Kurds and Circassians—Muslims unlikely to conspire with the foreigner. Although the evidence of Armenian terrorism is threadbare, it is repeated to this day by public figures in Turkey and in Turkish historical scholarship. As recently as 1990, a volume edited by a member of the Turkish Historical Society and bearing the title *British Documents on Ottoman Armenians* contained this editorial comment:

The principal aim of the Sassun insurgents was to secure the intervention of the Great Powers in favor of the Ottoman Armenians. The rebellion gave rise to much anti-Turkish propaganda in European countries. Public opinion in

Europe, particularly in Britain, was stirred up; there was a repetition of the outcry that had gone up after the Bulgarian insurrection of 1876. The Turcophobes of Europe and America started a campaign to persuade their Governments to exert diplomatic pressure on the Ottoman Government in an attempt to compel the Porte to give in to Armenian demands.

From the Armenian point of view, all this was another triumph for their network of revolutionary propaganda which they had systematically organized to provoke European reactions against Turkey.

The Armenian revolutionaries were doing their best to procure the intervention of the Powers by provoking all kinds of incidents throughout Anatolia, and in all of these incidents the aggressors were Armenians."[15]

This relentless and unbending view of what befell the Armenians of the Ottoman Empire has never changed in Turkish scholarship or in the statements of public figures in Turkey, despite the huge store of testimony from eyewitnesses. Thus, as mentioned in the introduction, two hostile groups of scholars representing diametrically opposed viewpoints confront the student keen to learn something of the relations between Ottomans and Armenians at the turn of the century. On one side, Armenian literature gives the picture of an innocent nation duped by cynically delivered promises from abroad while being left at the mercy of sadistic killers. On the other side, Turkey and her supporters claim that a genocide against the Armenians never took place.

The debate has become so vehement that Bernard Lewis, the dean of Middle Eastern historians in the United States, was recently sued in France by two organizations for denying (in an interview with *Le Temps* in November 1993) that there was a genocide against the Armenians. Nobody, including Lewis, denies that unpleasant events took place in the Ottoman Empire during the First World War, but Lewis argues that in no sense was there a genocide systematically organized from the center of the regime. There were simply local and sporadic initiatives undertaken by groups of Turks whose passions had become inflamed in the highly sensitive conditions of war. In any event, so these apologists for Turkey maintain, the Armenians gave as good as they got. Lewis claims that evidence of a conspiracy is not supported by the official documents. The problem is that these very documents have been suppressed by the Turkish establishment. Fortunately, other documents have been brought to light, and these documents (to be examined later) demonstrate beyond reasonable doubt that the genocide of the First World War was centrally organized.

Armenians were among the many citizens of the Ottoman Empire who, in the 1890s and early 1900s, forsook the stifling atmosphere of Abdülhamīd's police state for the freer climate of Paris, Geneva, or London. Many patriotic Turks as well saw the gradual erosion of their empire and believed that Abdülhamīd's policy of dissembling and delay simply no longer worked. Whatever his intentions may have been, Abdülhamīd was selling out to the foreigner, or so these Turks believed. They saw no diminution of foreign influence in the empire, so they made their way to the cities of Western Europe. Here they would meet, publicize, discuss, and work for some revised form of Ottomanism. All felt that the empire was disintegrating. They must salvage what they could.

They sent materials expressing their views back home through foreign-operated post offices. That was the only way leaflets, tracts, and all other instruments of what the sultan regarded as sedition could enter the country because of the sultan's vast system of censorship. Under a set of rules known as the Capitulations, foreigners living in the empire were exempt from trial in Ottoman courts; they maintained their own postal systems in which Ottoman censorship did not apply. This did not prevent the sultan's spies from maintaining a vigil outside each foreign-operated post office. A careful watch was kept on who entered or left such buildings. Ottoman citizens seen around these post offices were likely to be jailed or banished.

It was clear that if change were to come within the empire, it could hardly originate with the Turkish peasants in Anatolia. This heartland of Turkish settlement, beloved by sultans (because of the peasants' unquestioning loyalty) and by many English scholars and aesthetes (because the peasants represented the "simple" virtues in a Europe that was rapidly becoming too commercialized for their tastes), had not changed its views for centuries. It was the bedrock of the Ottomans. The peasants there were almost universally illiterate and had done what they had been told since time immemorial.

Consequently, since there was no large pool within the Turkish community from which a grassroots revolution could have sprung, it was among the newer entrants into an emerging middle class that the first stirrings of dissidence became manifest. The opportunities for an ambitious Turk, even of good family, were limited to public service of some type, either in the army, the navy, or the government bureaucracy. There were no institutes of higher learning at which such a Turk's horizons might be stretched. The only schools of any sophistication were those reluctantly founded by Abdülhamīd. As we have seen, the sultan found himself in a bind. He knew that somehow his defunct empire must take what it could from Europe in the areas of science and military studies. But would the process stop there? Was it possible to expose the brighter Turkish students to European methodologies without their acquiring, along the way, a deepening interest in politics? Would he not in this way encourage radicalism? Events were to prove that his anxieties were well founded.

In the military medical school, for example, to which some of the more astute brains had been attracted, the earliest meetings of the Young Turks took place. Soon the word had spread to the military academy itself, to the veterinary school, and to the civil college, at which those entering the government service were educated. At all of these institutions, young, forceful, and ambitious Turks—who considered themselves first and foremost patriots—gathered in secret and discussed the future. Those with resources took the opportunity offered by study abroad to escape the constraints of a police state. Such a person was Dr. Nazim, in due course one of the Young Turks' most sinister leaders, who went to Paris to study medicine and to conspire with his peers.

The Young Turks abroad took what appealed to them from Western scholarship and philosophical discussion. Some came under the influence of Émile Durkheim, France's leading sociologist. If a science that applied to society could be developed, it was possible, so these Young Turks thought, to use it in their assessment of the future of the Ottomans.

A representative of the more liberal wing of the Young Turk movement at this time was Prince Sabaheddin. A member of the Ottoman royal family, he fled the empire in 1899, settled in Geneva, and espoused the cause of decentralization of the Empire. This was a cause close to the heart of all minorities, including the Armenians, because decentralization would bring with it a degree of local autonomy, which was precisely what they wanted. But the prince was fairly isolated in this idea. More European than many Europeans, speaking faultless French and with a penchant for English tailoring, the prince was abandoned by the majority of the Young Turks, who insisted that if the Ottomans had any future, it must be a future guaranteed by a strong central state. Otherwise, they argued, the Young Turk movement would remain at the mercy of those minorities their ancestors had acquired by conquest, minorities that invariably ended up deserting them. Young Turk conspirators at home and abroad began to unite on the principle that whatever rights minorities might enjoy (of religious practice, for example, or of assembly), the Armenians, Jews, Albanians, Bulgars, or members of any number of Christian sects were equal partners with them in one endeavor only: to topple Abdülhamīd.

In 1895 Ahmed Riza, long-time publicist abroad for the Young Turk cause, issued a program in which he stated categorically, "We wish to advance in the path of civilization but we declare resolutely we do not wish to advance other than in fortifying the Ottoman element."[16]

Did the Armenian political leadership take this kind of statement seriously? There must surely have been some among them who read the following statement with misgiving. It was penned in June of 1897 by Murat Bey, another Young Turk leader living abroad: "Assuredly a special Armenian question outside of the question of general reforms in Turkey, must not and cannot be raised, for the excellent reason that not a single basis whatsoever exists for the erection, even artificial, of an Armenia."[17] This, written after the 1894–96 slaughter of the Armenians, shows absolutely no remorse and underlines the fact that the Young Turks were not prepared to consider any Armenian efforts at independence. "The Armenians," continued

Murat Bey in the same article, "wish with true naiveté to cause a new Armenia to arise from the debris of the present Ottoman Empire. This idée fixe, this maladroit project, pushes them to criminal resolutions . . . with the unique purpose of exciting the susceptibilities of Moslems. But they are past masters in the practice of deceit and their maladroit and impossible manners, which give rise to the expression 'Armenianism,' aid them admirably to this end."

The depth of the hatred evinced by these words gives some indication of the feelings of the Young Turks toward the Armenians. The Armenians had courted foreign sponsorship, so they were now the Turks' enemy. The Armenian leaders, so enmeshed in their pursuit of help from abroad, displayed an almost blithe disregard for the fate of the Armenian masses. According to the Young Turk leaders, the Armenian activists were prepared to surrender huge numbers of their co-nationals to win foreign sympathy and, ultimately, Armenian independence. Here is one scholar's assessment of their policies in this regard: "The severity with which the Armenians were treated cannot be condoned, but it is equally difficult to condone the cold-blooded calculation with which the Armenian revolutionaries offered up thousands of their people in a vain attempt to achieve their ends."[18]

This is a curious evaluation. The Armenians in the empire were being murdered simply for being Armenian. Was it doubly intransigent of them to seek aid elsewhere? One commentator, generally sympathetic to the Armenian point of view, has maintained that "quantitatively there was nothing to chose between a long drawn out massacre or a quick one. Armenians died whether the government pursued its usual course of malevolence and corruption, or whether it tightened its organization and undertook a mass killing. Almost all of the massacres of the 1890s occurred without provocation; and to blame Armenian revolutionaries for the killings which occurred after the action of a revolutionary . . . is to confuse provocation with executive decision."[19] Did Armenian strategists perform the cruel arithmetic suggested by the Turks? Did they cynically decide that to make a more striking showing abroad (where it counted), huge numbers of Armenians must be sacrificed? It is clear that within the constraints in which they operated, they were in a you-will-be-slaughtered-if-you-do-and-slaughtered-if-you-don't situation.

Many Armenian activists might have accepted a piecemeal approach in which the Ottoman rulers might introduce some form of autonomy. But sentiment within the Young Turk movement was hardening. Gradually, the disparate sections of this group began to agree on one point; their base would be ethnocentric. As for the Armenians, they had no recourse but to appeal to powerful foreigners, even though this had the effect of inflaming the hatred of Young Turks.

To these Turkish patriots, it seemed as if every minority within their seemingly moribund and tottering empire had its foreign protector. Only the Turks themselves were exempt from this patronage.

The polarization increased. Turkish patriots drew more and more to the racist thinking manifested in the repression of the Armenians in the mid-1890s. The Armenians continued their efforts to get help from abroad.

Among their most impressive achievements was the foundation in Paris, in 1900, of a magazine entitled *Pro-Armenia*. It was not the first journal in the French language to espouse the cause of Armenian independence, but its founders were among the most illustrious French citizens of the time. On the editorial board were Georges Clemenceau, Anatole France, and Jean Jaurès. Once support of this caliber was granted to those whom the Young Turks increasingly came to view as their bitterest enemies, the Turks adopted more and more the colors of ethnocentrism.

To eradicate any ambiguity in this situation, Talaat, the most important spokesperson of the Committee of Union and Progress, announced the following in Salonika (now Thessaloníki) at the 1910 annual congress: "There can be no question of equality [for minorities] until we have concluded our task of Ottomanizing the Empire."

Chapter 3

YOUNG TURKS
AT THE HELM

When the Young Turks staged their revolution in 1908, the diplomatic establishment in Constantinople had very mixed information about their aims. Most of the embassies had on their staff a dragoman, a person versed in the language and customs of the Ottomans. These interpreters varied considerably in their ability to judge events. The Russian embassy was fortunate to have the services, in this capacity, of Andre Mandelstamm, an astute, thoughtful man who was later to write a history of the period. The British embassy was not so fortunate. Its dragoman was Gerald Fitzmaurice, who often allowed his prejudices to cloud his views. Intensely Catholic, anti-Semitic, and convinced that historical change came about only as a result of competing conspiracies between small groups lusting after power, Fitzmaurice was dispatched to Salonika to find out about the Young Turks. It was known that the Young Turks had a considerable foothold in this city. At Salonika, Fitzmaurice made his inquiries, sniffed around, and returned to Constantinople with the opinion that the Young Turk movement was a "Judeo-Masonic conspiracy."

In Fitzmaurice's defense, it must be pointed out that there was a large Jewish community at Salonika, mostly consisting of Sephardic Jews who had fled Spain during the Inquisition at the end of the fifteenth century. It is also true that in their attempt to hide their activities from Abdülhamīd's police spies, the Young Turks had acted with the kind of secrecy they had noted in the activities of the Freemasons. But here any similarity ended. The Young Turk movement derived most of its power and most of its following from the junior officers of army units away from the capital. Thus it was that when on July 21, 1908, the Young Turks, through their Committee of Union and Progress, sent a telegram to Sultan Abdülhamīd demanding the restoration of the constitution, it was junior officers of the regular Turkish army who were responsible for its dispatch. These officers were attached to the army stationed in Macedonia. When Abdülhamīd's response was to send some of his loyal troops to Salonika to bring these dissident officers to heel, it was these very army units under Enver Pasha who arranged to have the commanding officer of the sultan's force shot. Most of the sultan's troops, having not been paid for months and disillusioned with the results of Abdülhamīd's policies, joined the rebels. Abdülhamīd was forced to reintroduce the constitution, and he became a constitutional monarch.

It was the end of a frightful era in Ottoman history. The cramped, scheming, and dissembling behavior of Abdülhamīd, with its attendant nexus of police spies and informers all in his pay, had dominated life in the empire for more than a generation. In the euphoria that followed Abdülhamīd's loss of power,

Sultan Abdülhamīd, 1842–1918, often described as the
Red Sultan, because of the blood he caused to flow.
(Ullstein)

amazing scenes took place. Turks joined arms with Armenians
and jointly heralded a new era, an era in which the qualities
and potential of the Ottomans might finally be given expression. "Henceforth we are all brothers," declared Enver, "there
are no longer Bulgars, Greeks, Romanians, Jews, Moslems; under the same blue sky we glory in being Ottomans."

Although there is no mention of Armenians in Enver's list, the abundant optimism of the moment led even to a joint congregation of Turks and Armenians listening to Islamic and Christian prayers in a Christian cemetery, during a service of memorial for Armenians slaughtered in the massacres of the 1890s. It is understandable that Armenians might have indulged themselves with the thought that after all the killing, a new age was indeed about to dawn. And in fact, a brief honeymoon did take place at this time between the Young Turks and those minorities (Jews, Greeks, Armenians) who also believed that their lot might be improved if representative government were introduced.

This self-indulgence was short-lived. The Young Turk revolution did not usher in a new age; indeed, within a short while, conflicting elements within the empire began to reassert themselves. Large numbers of Ottomans knew that the Young Turks were basically anticlerical. It was, in the view of many *Ittihadists*, religion that had kept the empire back and that always got in the way of progress. Within a few weeks of the Young Turks' unseating of the sultan, religious elements within the population, goaded on by *softas* (students for the priesthood), began to make a play for a return to fundamentalist Islamism, to what they felt was the true way. Within the army itself, these elements had a considerable following. Soon after the revolution, troops of the 1st Army Corps mutinied. They overpowered their officers and, according to one commentator, "marched to the Aya Sophia Square near Parliament demanding the restoration of the Sheriat [the Sharia] . . . In the Chamber there was chaos. Committee of Union and Progress deputies fled for fear of their lives, and softas and soldiers were everywhere."[1] The youthfulness of the Young Turk army leaders offended the more reactionary army cadres. There were complaints that insufficient time was being allowed for prayers and that recruits were being sworn in by "mere boys." Only nine months after the Young Turk revolution, in April 1909, the reactionary elements in the empire combined and staged a counterrevolution at whose head was the scheming and intransigent sultan Abdülhamīd. This counterrevolution was conducted under the banner of a restoration of the Sharia, or sacred law. A huge crowd assembled in front of the Chamber of Deputies, and there were cries not only of "Down with the Constitution!" but of "Down with the Committee!" The Young Turks were saved only when Enver led units of the 3rd Army—an army that called itself an army of liberation—to Constantinople to quell the counterrevolution. This time Abdülhamīd was banished, and his brother was appointed sultan. Such military actions, in which Enver led army units faithful to the Committee of Union and Progress to redress a situation in the committee's favor, became a regular feature of Young Turk rule.

While versed in military command, the vocal elements within the Young Turk movement, the junior officers, had no experience in government. They were astute enough to build up a carefully organized following for the *Ittihad ve Teraki* throughout the empire, but the day-to-day work in parliament had to be left to those who were old enough to have had some political experience.

Although the counterrevolution was suppressed in Constantinople, the sudden reemergence of Islamism had an almost immediate effect elsewhere, especially in Cilicia. Here, on the Mediterranean, Armenians constituted about one-fifth of the population, with some eighty thousand persons. From April 13 to 15, 1909, anti-Armenian demonstrations were staged in Adana without any intervention by the forces of law and order. When the Young Turks had stabilized the situation in Constantinople, two regiments loyal to them were dispatched to Adana to quell the disturbances. But on April 24, shortly after the arrival of these regiments, renewed shooting broke out, and eyewitnesses testified that regular army units opened fire on the densely populated Armenian quarter, hurled firebombs into it, and set gasoline containers on fire at its peripheries. Some two hundred small Armenian villages in the area were also burned and plundered. The number of Armenian deaths was estimated to be some thirty thousand. It is still not clear whether these actions took place despite the intervention of the government, or on its authority. A special enquiry initiated in Constantinople in the month following the action failed to uncover any definite cause. The eventual punishment of thirty-four Turks and six Armenians can be regarded as only a sop to prevent foreign criticism. One scholar has commented, "Nobody at the time wanted to embarrass the Young Turks, who had only just dealt with the reactionary forces."[2]

There was a breathlessness about Young Turk activity between the revolution of 1908 and the outbreak of the First World War in 1914. There was little unanimity of purpose within the party itself. Keeping the dissident voters within their own party at bay required all the skills that Talaat rapidly acquired in his translation from post office worker and cipher clerk to party secretary and eventually minister of the interior. The rapid succession of shattering events on the international stage gave the party administration little opportunity to implement a recognizable party program. The leaders were forced simply to react to daily events. A brief summary of these events gives abundant examples of the pressures they faced: Spectacular defeats were sustained by the Turkish army in two wars with Bulgaria. Other Ottoman possessions in the Balkans, such as Bosnia and Herzegovina, were summarily taken over by Austria-Hungary. In 1911, there was war with Italy over Libya, and in 1912, with a combined force of Balkan powers. As a result, between 1908 and 1914 the empire lost 424,000 square miles of territory and some 5 million persons out of its population of 24 million. These were hardly circumstances in which a coherent policy of modernization could be launched.

Regardless of these external pressures, there were aspects of life that the administration endeavored to reform. One scholar summarizes the accomplishments of the Young Turks as follows:

> They established a new system of provincial and local administration. They modernized that of Constantinople itself, through a new municipal organization with an energetic program of public works, equipping it with such amenities as fire brigades and public transport services. They reorganized its police, together with that of the provinces, where the new-style gendarmerie, introduced into Macedonia by Abdul Hamid [Abdülhamīd], was extended to other parts of the Empire. . . . They tackled judicial reform. They expanded public education at all levels and for the first time opened the schools and the University of Constantinople to women. This move towards feminine emancipation was to lead, during the years ahead, to their entry into professional life and to new legislation with regard to the rights of the female sex.[3]

Despite these clearly worthwhile initiatives, the ineluctable polarization of Turks and Armenians continued apace. Between the 1909 mass slaughter in Cilicia and the outbreak of the First World War, there was an unremitting series of local attacks against Armenians in most areas of the empire. Individually or in small groups, Armenians were killed or raped and their possessions stolen.

The response of Armenian leaders was to keep the foreign diplomatic establishment informed. Armenian ecclesiastics and activists kept a running tally of these offenses. Details were methodically circulated to the consulates of the foreign powers, and these reports found their way to the embassies at Constantinople. In this way, Armenian leaders hoped to stimulate foreign sponsorship of the Armenian cause. It is difficult to see what else they could have done, in view of the continuous failure of the *Ittihadist* regime to afford protection of Armenian life and limb. The activities of these Armenian activists are documented in huge quantities of diplomatic memoranda, messages, and papers now available for study.[4]

On January 30, 1913, for example, the Austrian consul at Trebizond informed Vienna: "The question of Anatolian reform is on everybody's mind. . . . I consulted with several more or less revolutionary spirits [Armenian activists], asking them what they actually wanted. All agreed they needed a guarantee for their lives and property, something which does not yet exist . . . and in this connection they demand, first and foremost, the subjection of Armenian areas to foreign control. But this should be arranged through all the European states and not via Russia alone. . . . Only if the other European states fail to act would the Armenians be compelled to rely exclusively on the neighboring state of Russia."[5]

This succinctly summarizes the position of the Armenian leadership. Since Russia was the longtime enemy of the Turks, the Armenians knew they should avoid ending up in the Russian camp, because this would only antagonize the Turks. But as discussed in the previous chapter, the overriding question was how to protect life and property. If the other foreign powers did not respond to support their cause, the Armenians would be forced into the arms of Russia. (That the Armenians felt they had a knife at their throats must be borne in mind when assessing the actions of their leadership, which have often been viewed critically.)

The foreign powers were animated solely by self-interest. This included Russia, which had more to gain than the others and so evinced a repeated interest in the Armenians. On January 11, 1913, the Austro-Hungarian ambassador at Saint Petersburg advised Vienna that the Russian foreign minister had "informed me he had received very bad news from Armenia where, according to reports from Russian consulates situated there, the authorities had supplied the Kurds with weapons. Under no circumstances could Russia, with her obligation to protect the Christians of the Orient, tolerate a repetition of the Armenian massacres."[6]

It was thus on Russian initiative that an attempt was made among the foreign powers to carve out a strategy with the Young Turks that might rescue the situation for the Armenians. In the final years leading up to the First World War, therefore, a series of meetings and exchanges between members of the diplomatic establishment at Constantinople turned on the question of placing foreign inspectors in the Armenian *vilayets* to supervise and control the situation there. It was put forth that this must be achieved with the cooperation of the leading members of the Committee of Union and Progress.

Before we view this process sympathetically, however, it must be stressed that the diplomats did not relinquish their countries' best interests as a basis for their recommendations, and continued to be dominated by general feelings of paranoia. For example, "Wangenheim informed me in all secrecy," wrote the Austro-Hungarian ambassador at the Sublime Porte to Vienna on September 11, 1913, "that he had advised Berlin it was in Germany's interest to behave in such a way that the rejection of the Russian plan—with which Your Excellency knows the Armenians have associated themselves—does not come from the German Government. He told them Germany should wait until the plan is rejected by some other Power. This is not to protect Russian sensibilities, but so that the Armenians have no grounds to complain about German policy."[7]

Meanwhile from all corners of the globe efforts were made to urge the powers to intercede on behalf of the Armenians. From Bukovina in the Austro-Hungarian Empire, the local Armenian community pleaded with the foreign office in Vienna: "The introduction of the Constitution in Turkey awoke the hope among Armenians that for them too, an era of justice might be inaugurated. But despite their loyalty and devotion to the Ottoman cause, Armenians remain the victims of persecution by Kurds, and of the bloodbath of Adana [a reference to the events in Cilicia in 1909], even more frightful than those perpetrated under the Hamidian regime."[8] From far off Manchester in England, an appeal was made to Emperor Francis Joseph in Vienna to help the Armenians.

In February 1914, after many months of snail-paced progress, Russia and the Young Turk leaders signed an agreement accepted by the other powers. It provided for the division of Turkish Armenia into two administrative zones. One would cover the *vilayets* of Erzurum, Sivas, and Trebizond; the other, those of Van, Bitlis, Kharput, and Diarbekir. In conjunction with the Sublime Porte, the European powers would appoint to each area a foreign inspector general who would have overriding authority.

Some Armenian leaders counseled a wait-and-see attitude to this arrangement, but most saw it as a step in the right direction. They viewed the existence of foreign eyes in the right places, empowered to act, as at least a partial guarantee of Armenian security.

Several more months were required before the signatories could agree on the nominations for these posts. Finally, in April 1914, an erstwhile administrator from the Dutch East Indies named Westerenk and a Norwegian army officer named Hoff were appointed.

Whatever hopes kindled by this arrangement were quickly dowsed when the First World War broke out, for the signatories of the agreement were now on opposing sides. The project was stillborn.

Chapter 4

WHICH WAY WILL TURKEY GO?

During the spring and summer of 1914, war seemed imminent and the triumvirate that ruled the Ottomans cast about for the best system of alliances they might pursue. In this, the only constant factor was Enver, who never departed from his preference for a link with Germany. Such a move would place the Turks in an alliance with the Central Powers (Germany and Austria-Hungary) in the event of conflict.

It is interesting to speculate how the new rulers of the Ottomans, persons generally of humble background, coped with the niceties of diplomatic activity. They were forced to pick up quickly some knowledge of French, which was then the language of international diplomacy. But there were far more formidable obstacles. Among the European powers, a career in diplomacy was normally an avenue open only to persons with a title and an independent income—persons who were conscious of breeding and background.

Enver's origins, in contrast, were obscure. It is believed he was the son of a railway porter, but nourished by his almost Napoleonic ambitions, Enver had managed not only to become minister of war, but also to marry a royal princess, thereby earning for himself the title of damad.

Talaat, arguably the most gifted of the three and the only civilian, liked to consider himself a man of the people. He had peasant origins, and it was thought that he had gypsy blood in his veins. Although originally a letter carrier and telegraph operator, his remarkable talent for negotiation and persuasion and his earthy amiability (which intrigued several diplomats) vaulted him to the role of the chief architect of the fortunes of the Young Turks.

Ahmed Djemal, the least public of the triumvirs, was a 1895 product of the staff college and came from a military family. He saw service, like so many of the Young Turks, with the 3rd Army at Salonika, where he came under the influence of the Committee of Union and Progress. When he was appointed inspector of railways, he used his newfound mobility to spread the *Ittihadist* gospel. Short, bearded, energetic, and uncompromising, he had in 1908 become a member of the Executive Committee of the party and, as one of its leaders, played a prominent role in suppressing the counterrevolution of 1909. In the work of suppression he displayed toughness and dedication, and he was rewarded by the party with the governorship of that section of Constantinople on the Asian side of the Bosporus. Later he became governor of Adana, and in 1911, of Baghdad. After the coup d'état of January 13, 1914 (in which, shortly after Liman's arrival, Enver appointed himself minister of war), he was appointed governor and military chief of Constantinople and in this capacity he rooted out any opposition to the regime of the triumvirate. If decisive and uncompromising action was needed, Djemal was the man.

Weakened by numerous military defeats, their economy continually on the verge of bankruptcy, and at the mercy of independence movements throughout their empire, the Young Turk leaders appreciated that their short- and long-term survival depended on having a strong ally. They were not governed by any ideological considerations. The yardstick was always the same: Where can we exact the maximum advantage? What they had to offer, basically, were the precious Straits (including the Dardanelles and Bosporus straits), an area the Russians desperately wanted to control. The Straits also were a key to the decisions of the British, keen to ensure that the land route to their empire in India did not fall into the hands of potential enemies. It was also vital to the British that the sea route via Suez remain open.

Given this situation, Djemal favored a rapprochement with France. He was not as persuaded as Enver about the superiority of German arms. In the spring of 1914, he traveled to Paris to try to negotiate terms. Once in Paris, he found that the French were playing a waiting game. They could not, so they argued, make any arrangement with the Ottomans unless the other members of the Triple Entente (Russia and England), with whom they were bound by treaty, came in too. But having made this point, the French seemed disinclined to approach their allies. Djemal returned to Constantinople with the impression that he had been fobbed off.

From Russia, however, the auguries were much more promising. In May 1914, Saint Petersburg even suggested to the Ottomans an agreement in the event of hostilities. Should Turkey be attacked, so Russia proposed, its security would be guaranteed by Russia. In return, Turkey would close the Straits to all enemy powers. Once the Germans had been defeated, ran the Russian proposal, all German possessions in Asia would be ceded to Turkey. Though these ideas emanated from Turkey's historical foe, Talaat thought they offered the best alternative, and he went immediately to Saint Petersburg to propose a formal alliance. But negotiations foundered, and Talaat returned to Constantinople empty-handed.

The Young Turks had repeatedly initiated talks with the British, but these had received little or no encouragement from London. Nothing, therefore, stood in the way of a deal with the Central Powers; in any event, Enver had continuously been in favor of it. He did not permit his increasingly worsening relations with Liman von Sanders to deflect him.

Another group watched, with bated breath, the events of that summer. The Armenian political leaders viewed all this diplomatic activity with great anxiety; their own political needs had been placed on a back burner by all the powers, whose policy makers were now occupied with more urgent considerations.

The only possible outcome that might work to Armenian advantage was if the Ottomans allied themselves with Russia. Given the distribution of Armenian populations between the Ottoman Empire and tsarist Russia, conflict between these two could only imperil the Armenian situation. It is estimated that, at the time, some 2,076,000 Armenians lived in the Ottoman Empire, about 2,054,000 in the Russian Empire, and an additional 390,000 in the other countries of the world. In the opinion of the Armenian political leaders, to push for Ottoman neutrality or a Russian alliance with Turkey was the only way to avoid a bloodbath.

Nowhere were the huge issues surrounding the First World War debated with more intensity than at the last prewar conference of the *Dashnakstutium* party at Erzurum, which took place in July 1914.

The Armenian presence had always been very strong in the *vilayet* of Erzurum. This area, close to the border between the Ottoman and Russian Empires, which had shifted regularly according to the fortunes of war, was always under Ottoman military surveillance. The Russians, too, maintained considerable military intelligence there.

The actual prewar Armenian population figures in this *vilayet* are generally in dispute because Turkey maintained at the postwar peace conference that Armenian claims to the area had been bolstered by their tampering with population statistics. Nonetheless, even Turkish statistics allow for some 137,000 Armenians in this *vilayet,* and even though this is some 60,000 fewer than what is claimed by the Armenian leaders, it still shows a substantial Armenian presence.[1]

The *Dashnakstutium* party was the largest of the Armenian political organizations. Choosing to hold the meeting in the city of Erzurum, close to the border, made it accessible to Armenians of both the Ottoman and the Russian Empires. It is not difficult to imagine the state of tension, the explosive nature of the debates, that must have typified the sessions of that congress: Which way would Turkey go? There were members whose families had already made the move to Russia to escape the persecutions of the Abdülhamīd era. It can hardly be denied that feelings toward the Ottomans were far from cordial, even though at the time the Armenians had fourteen representatives in the Ottoman parliament. This institution had become more and more titular in its power, since events were controlled behind the scenes by the Central Committee of the Committee of Union and Progress.

Shortly before the congress ended, Armenian leaders, who had not yet packed up to leave, were surprised by a visit from a small delegation of *Ittihadists*.

At its head was Behaeddin Shakir, a member of the Central Committee and a man known only as one of the behind-the-scenes operators of the *Ittihadists*. Shakir announced that he had come with some proposals for the Armenians to consider.

In the event of conflict between the Ottomans and Russians, said Shakir, the *Dashnaks* should arrange for their supporters across the border to ease the path of Turkish army units. They should foment rebellion, give the Russian units false information, and generally aid the cause of Turkish arms in what was very familiar country to them.

There would be rewards, continued Shakir. On the successful conclusion of the campaign against Russia, the Ottomans would cede to the Armenians all of Russian Armenia and, for good measure, would throw in areas of Erzurum, Bitlis, and Van (areas of heavy Armenian settlement).

By the way, added Shakir, the *Ittihadists* had made similar proposals to other minorities in the Caucasus, such as the Georgians and Azerbaijanis. These minorities had, he told the Armenians, assured the Ottomans of their cooperation.

Shakir was a bitter enemy of the Armenians. He would be one of the prime agents in their slaughter. It is difficult to resist the thought that he must have enjoyed the tense atmosphere his offer undoubtedly created. We need only think back to the intensity of the hatred demonstrated by the Young Turks in exile toward the Armenians, a hatred that animated Shakir in his subsequent actions.

The *Dashnak* leaders, in fact, did not quite know how to reply to this offer. It would be wrong to assume they had abandoned any feeling of solidarity with the notion of Ottomanism, despite the long history of persecution they had endured. They eventually blurted out an answer based on the premise that it was in the Ottomans' best interests to pursue a policy of neutrality; in any event, they assured Shakir, they would remain totally loyal to the Ottoman cause. Since they had been given the right to bear arms, they had demonstrated their value in battle, and the Ottomans could count on them again.

Armenians had been allowed to bear arms and enter the army only since the revolution of 1908, and they had demonstrated great fighting abilities as frontline soldiers in the Balkan wars. And when the Ottomans did enter World War I on the side of the Central Powers, prayers for an Ottoman victory became part of the church schedule in Armenian churches. It was, after all, Enver himself who wrote to the Armenian archbishop of Konya shortly after the outbreak of the war, "I am glad to use this opportunity to confirm that Armenian soldiers of the Ottoman army have performed their duties in the theatre of war, very conscientiously. I can verify this from personal experience. I would ask you to convey to the Armenian nation, known for its dedication to the Ottoman cause, my satisfaction and gratitude."[2]

This statement must be viewed in its proper context, however. It comes from a man who only a few months earlier had set up an organization headed by Shakir, whose function was to eliminate the Armenians from the map of Turkey.

As far as the Armenians in Russia were concerned, it was the Ottomans who had slaughtered their fellow Armenians under Abdülhamīd and who had followed this up with the massacres in Cilicia in 1909. Armenians in Russia enlisted in large numbers in tsarist forces; there is little doubt they were joined by volunteers from Turkey. Four corps of Armenian volunteers were formed, and they were very shortly fully subscribed. This voluntary enlistment is the basis for the Turkish arguments that the Armenians were disloyal during the First World War.

Meanwhile no fewer than forty thousand Armenians enrolled in the Ottoman army and pledged allegiance to the Ottoman cause. The awful situation that Armenian leaders most wanted to avoid had come to pass. There were thousands of Armenians wearing Russian uniforms on one side of the frontier, and thousands wearing Turkish ones on the other. It does not require much imagination to determine the uses the Young Turks might make of this situation. As one of the leading authorities on modern Armenian history has assured us, "It is noteworthy that Hovannes Kachaznuni and Simon Vratzian, the first and last premiers of the future [Armenian] Republic, warned that the *Ittihadist* rulers of Turkey would utilize the existence of volunteer units, composed partly of former Ottoman subjects, to justify violent measures against the Turkish Armenians."[3]

The misgivings of these future premiers were quickly justified.

The fate of the Armenian men in the Ottoman army was speedily settled. In the fall and winter of 1914, they were deprived of their arms and detailed to road-building work in the most primitive conditions, largely being used as pack animals. The death rate was accordingly very high. Those who survived would, in due course, be roped together and shot.

The Armenian leaders at Erzurum were not the only actors waiting to see which route the Young Turks might take. Liman von Sanders, head of the German military mission, spent

July of 1914 trying to sense the direction in which German policy was headed. He was certain that negotiations were taking place to which he was not privy. At the end of that fateful month, on the twenty-ninth of July, his government declared war on Russia. Liman was consumed by the notion that he was allowing these large events to pass him by. War is the locomotive on which military ambition is propelled, and Liman certainly did not want the great opportunities it offered to escape him.

Constantinople was rife with rumor. One day it was bruited about that Turkey would join the Entente of Britain, France, and Russia. The next it was rumored that it would ally with the Central Powers of Germany and Austria-Hungary.

Liman made renewed attempts to get himself and his fellow officers assigned to the European theater. On the third of August, Germany invaded Belgium; it had been clear since the murder of Austrian Archduke Francis Ferdinand on June 28 that Europe was a powder keg. The only positive aspect of this situation for a serving officer was that war meant rapid advancement. Liman sent a succession of cables to the military cabinet at home, but all his requests for reassignment were turned down. This was because, unbeknownst to him, negotiations for an alliance between Germany and the Ottomans were well under way, and the continued presence of the German military mission was considered vital.

It was not until the first days of August 1914 that Liman was put in the picture. He received a summons to visit Wangenheim at the German embassy. Here he found the ambassador in closed session with Enver. "They informed me," he was later to write, "they were considering the plan of a secret alliance between Germany and Turkey and desired my advice as to the employment of the military mission in case Turkey entered the war."[4] Liman's reply was characteristic of the man.

He said nothing about the defense of the Straits or how to capture Suez. His reply, as he described it after a lapse of some five years, was that in the event of such an alliance, "German officers should be assigned positions that would give them real influence on the conduct of the war."[5] Therefore, Liman missed a golden opportunity to demonstrate his keen appreciation of the tactical and logistic needs of the moment. Not for nothing did General Hans von Seeckt, Germany's leading officer in Turkey at the war's end, claim that Liman's appointment was nothing other than a catastrophe for German arms.

In fact, in early August 1914, within a very few days of Shakir's appearance at the *Dashnak* conference in Erzurum, a secret treaty was signed between Germany and Turkey. Enver then founded the organization called *Teshkilati Mahsusa* (Special Organization), whose function was to eliminate the Armenians of the Ottoman Empire. But it was not until October 30, 1914, that units of the Turkish navy (officered by Germans) provided a cause for the declaration of war on Russia by staging an incident on the Black Sea in which they were "forced" to bombard Russian ports.

In the meantime, the Germans had opportunity to consider firsthand what had to be done to enhance Turkish warreadiness. There were urgent problems of an economic nature to be addressed. The Turkish army was chronically short of equipment, especially armaments. To repair this situation, the Ottoman treasury had to be replenished. To the alarm of some German economists and bankers, Germany met a request from the *Ittihadists* for $20 million in gold, only to have Enver immediately ask for a second sum of the same size. The Ottoman treasury became a bottomless pit into which Germany would need repeatedly to pour gold; this had to be done if there was to be any advantage derived from the association so assiduously fostered by William II and Wangenheim.

In the same week that Enver wrote a letter to the Armenian archbishop of Konya praising his Armenian troops, he arranged through Talaat at the Ministry of the Interior to issue a decree ordering that "all Armenian soldiers are to be withdrawn from fighting positions and Armenian officials are to be withdrawn from office."[6] Since the Special Organization charged with eliminating the Armenians had already been founded, the preparations for the genocide that was to follow were now well under way.

The dearth of ammunition (Krupps in Germany was no longer prepared to provide armaments on credit) and the lack of transport facilities and other military necessities in no way dampened Enver's enthusiasm for risky military action. On December 6, 1914, he appeared in Liman's office.

Enver announced to a startled Liman that he was about to leave for Trebizond, whence he would personally take command of the 3rd Army. At its head, he would drive the Russians back over the Caucasus. He would then continue to Afghanistan, cross the northwest frontier, and challenge the British Empire in India. (This was all in keeping with Enver's dream of linking up en route with the various peoples whom he had designated as being of Turkic origin.)

A few days before this visit, Liman had received a report from a German officer stationed at Erzurum, on Enver's route to his proposed battlefield, in which he had been assured that the existing defenses would be powerless against a Russian assault. "The operation was difficult if not wholly impracticable," he later wrote. "According to the maps and everything I could learn of them, the roads in question were narrow mountain

roads or trails over high ridges. At that time they were probably deep in snow. . . . I called Enver's attention to these grave
objections, as was my duty."[7] Reading between the lines of
Liman's memoirs, it is possible to deduce that Liman's view of
Enver was that he was governed by six parts vanity to four parts
skill.

Nothing could stop Enver, however. He planned to attack
Sarikamish, where there was a Russian military base, then continue to Baku, seizing the fortress of Kars on the way, and at
Baku stage the first of a number of uprisings against the tsar
among the Muslim communities there. It was not until Christ-
mas Day of 1914 that Enver began his attack. But his army was
ill-prepared for a winter campaign in the snows of the Caucasus. Out of an army of some 100,000 men, about 90,000 are
estimated to have perished in the snow, against which their
threadbare uniforms offered no protection.

This catastrophic defeat, which all rational military analysis would have foreseen, is sometimes called the retreat from
Sarikamish.

It would have important repercussions on the war councils
of Russia and England.

Chapter 5

LONDON, JANUARY 1915

By December 1914, the fate of the Armenians of the Ottoman Empire could not have been further from the minds of the architects of Entente strategy. Nonetheless, Enver's defeat in the Caucasus set events in train that had the effect of putting further nails into the coffin of the Armenian nation.

These actions started in the mind of Grand Duke Nicholas, commander in chief of the forces of tsarist Russia. The grand duke was fighting a war on two fronts. To take some pressure off the French in the west, he had agreed, in the autumn of 1914, to attack the Germans in the east and attempt to overrun East Prussia. There he ran into the superb generalship of Paul von Hindenburg (only recently called out of retirement) and Erich Ludendorff, and his forces were routed. Although he had plenty of soldiers, the grand duke was severely short of armaments, and there was no way his allies could help him out. He was separated from them by a landmass in the hands of the enemy. How different the story might have been if Russia had controlled the Straits. Britain and France would have been able to send munitions across the Mediterranean to the Straits, proceed on through, and supply Russia through its Black Sea ports. This notion began to dog Nicholas's thinking.

The grand duke had better success against Enver. In the midst of his stunning victory over the Turks in the Caucasus, Nicholas arranged to send a memorandum to the British secretary of state for war, Lord Horatio Kitchener. In it he asked whether it would be possible "to stage a demonstration . . . either naval or military, and so to spread reports as to cause the Turks . . . to withdraw some of the forces now acting against the Russians in the Caucasus and thus ease the Russian position."[1] The message was sent via the British embassy in Saint Petersburg and was graced neither by an explanatory note from the ambassador, Sir George Buchanan, nor by an advisory from the British military attaché to take the request with a grain of salt. Was this, perhaps, because embassy officials believed that British intelligence was already aware of the total rout of the Turkish forces? There is no doubt that independent British intelligence in the Caucasus was well developed; many of the British consuls who had served in that area in the 1890s were part of the military.

In any event, given the complete defeat of Enver's 3rd Army, Nicholas's request is curious. There would always be a reason to help the Russians with armaments, but why now, in the light of the recent Russian victory, had the grand duke asked for a show of force? Even more curious is the fact that the British accepted the grand duke's request at face value. This raises a number of questions.

The men in question in London were members of a relatively new instrument of government called the War Council. It had been set up to deal with the emergency situation occasioned by the nature of trench warfare in the winter of 1914. The council consisted of the prime minister, the lord chancellor, the chancellor of the exchequer, the foreign minister, and the secretary of state for war. As its secretary, it employed Lieutenant Colonel (later Lord) Maurice Hankey. Occasionally, supplementary brass from the army and navy were called in so that the members might benefit from their expertise.

Because of his huge following throughout the country, Lord Kitchener was probably the council's most powerful member. He was England's most popular and most successful soldier. His grim countenance with its huge mustachio appeared in every village square over the slogan Your Country Needs You. (The English still resisted the idea of conscription into the forces; at this time, England had a volunteer army, at the nucleus of which was a group of highly trained professional soldiers.)

Kitchener's vast military experience, however, did not make him a good committee member. In fact, he was often given to silences of indeterminate origin. Some of his colleagues in the War Council were of the opinion that he withheld information from them, for reasons they thought whimsical. Most were prepared to tread carefully in his presence. Apart from his popularity, they understood that he had the well-nigh impossible job of replacing the huge casualties suffered by Sir John French's British Expeditionary Force in France and Flanders. It was these losses that so exercised the members of the council. The politicians needed a victory somewhere to buttress their standing in the country, while the soldiers and sailors had to do something to restore their rapidly tarnishing reputations.

The most dynamic member of the council was Winston Churchill, who occupied the post of first lord of the Admiralty.[2] Informed, hard working, incisive, and, above all, more articulate than any other member of the council, Churchill, then forty years old and at the height of his intellectual powers, enjoyed a mixed reception among his peers. Civilians generally revered him. Career officers in the army or navy, reared in the tradition of clipped sentences and understatement, frequently came to dislike Churchill, for the first lord of the Admiralty, who delivered silver-tongued oratory with great facility (a characteristic of politicians that most soldiers disliked), often seemed to pursue his own advantage in an obvious fashion. He was not, so they considered, one of them.

In a severe and highly charged stock-taking on the occasion of New Year's Eve 1914, the chancellor of the exchequer, David Lloyd George, wrote his thoughts down in a memorandum circulated to members of the council on New Year's Day. "We need a definite victory somewhere," he wrote. "Otherwise morale in France and Great Britain will suffer from the mounting casualty lists with few or no visible territorial gains to offset them."

This his colleagues already knew. But where? The victory was hardly likely to occur on the western front. Three hundred and fifty miles of trenches stretched from the English Channel to the Swiss frontier, their occupants bogged down in the mud, surviving what had already come to be considered the worst war of attrition in history.

By January 2, 1915, the War Council had been apprised of the telegram Kitchener had received from Grand Duke Nicholas. On that day, he replied to the Russians. He purposely left his recommendations as vague as possible. He told them a "demonstration would be made but this could not be counted on to relieve the Russian army in the Caucasus." The word *demonstration* is a good one to use to keep one's options open. A demonstration might be as superficial as a piece of gunboat diplomacy, such as sending a couple of battleships into the Straits and firing at the gun emplacements in the hope that the enemy would come to realize it faced an adversary too powerful to withstand. Or it might mean a number of other things, but in any event, a demonstration as a military device is somewhat anemic.

If Kitchener knew about the fate of the Turkish 3rd Army, he was prepared to pretend he did not. But he certainly kept his opposite number, Churchill at the Admiralty, informed about his exchange with the grand duke, for Churchill immediately discussed the matter with the first sea lord.[3] Lord John Fisher was a highly popular leading sailor known affectionately as Jackie Fisher, who had been cajoled by Churchill into returning to the service after his retirement. Fisher's instant reaction was to propose sending an army to the Dardanelles (the narrow sea approach, via the Sea of Marmara, to Constantinople itself). He argued that all the East Indian troops could be used as well as seventy-five thousand British troops, which might be landed on the eastern shores.

One wonders with what rage this advice was received by Kitchener, already scraping the barrel of British soldiers to supply replacements on the western front. This was a far cry from the notion of a demonstration, which was all he had committed himself to. The kind of involvement in the eastern Mediterranean proposed by Fisher would drain resources on the western front, which is where Kitchener and the other soldiers were convinced the war would be won or lost.

But what of the chances of an inexpensive naval action?

Never one to waste time, on January 3, 1915, Churchill cabled the commanding officer of Britain's fleet in the Aegean Sea. He asked if the Straits could be forced with old battleships.

To force them meant to send a sufficient supply of vessels, all firing rapidly at the gun emplacements as they proceeded through the narrows, in such strength as to overwhelm the enemy positions. If a sufficient number could get through, the exercise would be justifiable. And once they had got through, they would sail on to Constantinople, where the entire "rotten edifice" (for so it was characterized) of the Young Turk regime would come tumbling down. This view of the status of the Young Turk regime was not based on fantasy; the British were well aware through their network of informers of the precarious standing of the Young Turk rulers.

Churchill had to wait only two days for a reply from Admiral Sackville Carden, who headed the British fleet in the Aegean. In it he said, "While the Dardanelles cannot be rushed, they might be forced by extended operations with large numbers of ships." Churchill, whose day ended at 4:00 A.M. (exactly the time Lord Fisher's began), consulted with the brass at the Admiralty. On January 6, he advised Carden: "Your view is agreed with by high authorities here. Please telegraph in detail what you think could be done by extended operations, what force would be needed and how you consider it should be used."

Carden's response was to submit a plan to the Admiralty on January 11. He said he needed twelve battleships, three battle cruisers, and various smaller vessels. While there were several officers who thought that Churchill was proceeding with unseemly haste, they consoled themselves with the notion that in the event the scheme did not work, it could always be described afterward as simply an attempt that did not come off, or an initiative that masked some more important strategy elsewhere.

In any event, on the thirteenth of January 1915, the War Council wholeheartedly endorsed the idea of an assault on the

Dardanelles. Its secretary, Lieutenant Colonel Hankey, wrote in his memoirs: "The idea caught on at once. The whole atmosphere changed. Fatigue was forgotten. The War Council turned eagerly from the dreary vista of a slogging match on the Western Front to brighter prospects, as they seemed, in the Mediterranean."

As they seemed. But then, anything would have seemed brighter as an option than continued stalemate in France and Flanders. It was an irresistible idea and doubtless was made doubly attractive because of the bind these strategists were in. However, it must be mentioned that these high-ranking army and navy officers were hardly ignorant of the terrain of the Straits. In the declining years of the nineteenth century, enterprising officers at British military institutes had discussed and evaluated the feasibility of an invasion of Constantinople via the Straits. Almost overwhelmingly, expert military opinion was that it was not possible. One of the most recent studies was made by Colonel Chermside, an erstwhile British vice consul and later military attaché at the British embassy at Constantinople.

Colonel Chermside's study was dated November 15, 1895, and bore the title "The estimated capacity of Turkish Military Organization to reinforce the garrisons of the Dardanelles and Gallipoli Peninsula." In making his computations, the British officer assumed that communication by sea would be available to the Turks, in the absence of railroads or good roads, of which the empire was notoriously short. (The German engineers who were rapidly descending on Turkey were trying desperately to improve road conditions, but they could not be expected to work miracles.) Given transport by sea, Chermside reckoned that within one week the Turks could get 20,000 soldiers and 180 field guns there. If they did not have use of the sea lanes, this would be reduced to 9,000 to 10,000 soldiers and 84 field guns. However, within two weeks these figures would be increased to 37,200 and 180, respectively. Bearing in mind the notorious shortages within the Ottoman army, it is probable that Chermside's figures for guns were academic. One thing they did demonstrate, however, was that whatever the British intended to achieve in the Dardanelles, it had to be done quickly. "It is therefore very evident," Chermside summarized, "that Turkey could mobilize in a short time very large field forces on both sides of the Straits."[4]

These views (and those expressed in other studies) notwithstanding, the notion of forcing the Straits, rather than attempting to land a large force, was the one that obtained currency within the council. Had it been admitted that a larger military force was a precondition of success, the plan would have fallen foul of Lord Kitchener, nursing his virtually insoluble problems in the west. And had the plan's proponents demanded a much larger naval presence (using modern dreadnoughts rather than older vessels due to be scrapped), they would have had to deal with Lord Fisher and the establishment at the Admiralty. The proponents of the scheme were thus forced to act within these constraints.

"It was a gamble," wrote one commentator much later, "but it looked like an inexpensive one. The importance of Constantinople could not be exaggerated. There was no other city in the country to replace it; no network of roads and railways which would have enabled the army and the government to have rapidly regrouped in another place. The fall of Constantinople was in effect the fall of the state, even though resistance might have been maintained indefinitely in the mountains."[5]

Another feature of the operation was the almost total impossibility of making it a secret. At each of the hundreds of islands in the Aegean Sea, the presence of Ottoman (and now German) intelligence agents could be assumed. The assembly and progress of allied vessels would be public knowledge.

Bad weather prevented Admiral Carden from sending his ships into the Straits until the twenty-fifth of February. On this day, his second in command, Vice Admiral de Roebeck, in the *Vengeance*, bombarded the gun emplacements. The defending gunners, mostly Turks but with some Germans, quickly ran out of ammunition and retreated to the north. The weather remained uncertain. After the gunners on the shore had been silenced, the British sent some landing parties to investigate.

They discovered that the Turkish gun emplacements had been abandoned. As they moved deeper into the Straits, they met some fire from mobile howitzers provided by the Germans, but they sustained no damage.

On March 2, 1915, Carden cabled Churchill to the effect that if he were not let down by the weather, he should get to Constantinople in about two weeks.

It would be difficult to overestimate the feeling of joy and exultation this message conveyed to the dispirited politicians, soldiers, and sailors of the War Council. Lord Fisher, who had repeatedly expressed misgivings about the operation and even threatened to resign on this issue as recently as January 23, offered to rush out immediately and take over the command. In far-off Chicago, the price of grain fell; U.S. dealers reckoned on huge quantities of Russian grain entering the world market as a result of free Russian access to the Mediterranean.

But there was a problem. Having passed on the good news, Admiral Carden suffered an illness that some commentators claim was psychosomatic in nature and reflected his misgivings about the project. Some students of naval history still ask why the command was not passed to Admiral Limpus, the erstwhile leader of the British naval mission in Constantinople, who surely knew more about the defenses of the Dardanelles than any other serving British officer. In any event, the project was taken over by de Roebeck, who had been serving under Carden in the Aegean.

Carden's indisposition did not affect the feeling of optimism prevailing at the War Council. Its members were by now convinced that an inexpensive means (the vessels involved were due to be scrapped) had been discovered to deliver a blow to the Germans by silencing their new allies. And its propaganda value was immeasurable. In the Aegean Sea, British and French warships were rapidly assembled for the follow-up exercise that would deliver the *coup de grâce*.

During all these developments, British naval intelligence had not been inactive. Its director, Captain Reginald Hall, had long been of the opinion, backed up by reports from his intelligence sources in the region, that the Young Turks needed only the slightest of pushes to be removed from power. Captain Hall calculated that there were even less-expensive methods of hastening this process than the naval assault. On his own authority, without informing the British cabinet, the foreign office, or indeed his colleagues at the Admiralty, he opened negotiations with high-ranking officials at the Sublime Porte (including, as one rumor had it, with Talaat himself). If the Turks would withdraw from the war and give Allied vessels unimpeded access through the Straits to the Black Sea, Hall told them, they would receive £3 million (equivalent to $12 million in U.S. dollars).

As emissaries, he dispatched Edwin Whittle, George Eady, and none other than Gerald Fitzmaurice, erstwhile dragoman at the British embassy in Constantinople, to the town of Dedeagath in Thrace.[6] These negotiators were empowered to go up to £4 million ($16 million). However, should the Turks delay, the amount would be reduced daily until such time as an accommodation had been reached.[7] Hall's confidence in this scheme was bolstered when naval intelligence intercepted a signal from Constantinople to Berlin disclosing that the Turks were desperately short of ammunition. He had no doubt that he was striking while the iron was hot.

On the fifteenth of March the three emissaries landed at Dedeagath and opened negotiations with representatives of the Young Turk regime. Some progress was made, but the project foundered on one issue: London was unable to guarantee that Constantinople would remain in Turkish hands at the conclusion of the war. The Turkish delegates insisted on making this a precondition of any agreement. But Hall's inquiries showed the British foreign office to be immovable on this point; in fact, there had been an under-the-table agreement with Russia by the other members of the Entente that Russia should receive Constantinople after the war.

Meanwhile, further attacks of bad weather delayed de Roebeck's assault. It was not until March 18 that the Allied fleet set sail. This time they encountered a line of mines that aerial reconnaissance had failed to detect. One historian has written, "A Turkish mine expert had taken a small steamer called the *Nousret* down into Eren Keui Bay and there, parallel to the Asiatic shore and just inside the slack water, he had laid a new line of twenty mines. He did this because he had seen British warships maneuvering there during the previous day."[8]

The toll on the allied fleet was substantial. The *Bouvet* (French) and the *Irresistible* and *Ocean* (British) were sunk.

The effect on British military opinion, once the news reached London, was catastrophic. All those associated with the enterprise behaved as if they never really believed in its viability and had given their support only with profound misgivings. The new reasoning was that to continue without a large military landing force would compound the original error.

Only one voice continued to plead that the remaining ships should speed on to Constantinople. Only one voice urged anyone who would listen that in the appalling arithmetic of war, the losses sustained in the Straits so far were trifling compared with those that accrued daily on the western front. Churchill used every avenue at his command to continue the endeavor. He was certain that the Young Turk regime was at its last gasp; all intelligence pointed to this. But the military leadership had lost its appetite for the enterprise; Churchill's voice remained solitary. Only Roger Keyes, Carden's chief of staff, remained as convinced as Churchill that the attempt should continue. "I had a most indelible impression that we were in the presence of a beaten foe," he was later to write. "I thought he was beaten at 2 P.M. I knew he was beaten at 4 P.M.—and at midnight I knew with still greater certainty that he was absolutely beaten; and it only remained for us to organize a proper sweeping force and devise some means of dealing with the drifting mines to reap the fruits of our efforts. I felt that the guns of the forts and batteries and the concealed howitzers and mobile field guns were no longer a menace. Mines moored and drifting must, and could, be overcome."[9]

Then, on March 20, 1915, the *New York Times* carried the following story:

WHOLE PLAIN STREWN BY ARMENIAN BODIES.
TURKS AND KURDS REPORTED TO HAVE
MASSACRED MEN, WOMEN AND CHILDREN.

Appalling accounts of conditions in Armenia have reached
the officials in London of the Armenian Red Cross Fund.
. . . The plain of Alashgard is virtually covered with the bodies of men, women and children. . . .

Chapter 6

Constantinople, March 1915

Were Winston Churchill and Reginald Hall correct in their belief that the Young Turks were at the end of their tether? Memoirs written by various persons in privileged positions to gauge the situation suggest that they were.

Among these witnesses, the comments of Henry Morgenthau, the ambassador from the United States, are of considerable significance. Successful in business, Morgenthau had made a midcareer switch to government service. He decided at the age of fifty that he had achieved financial security. Impressed with Woodrow Wilson, he supported his presidential campaign and became one of its largest contributors. He hoped that if elected, Wilson would reward him with a cabinet office, if possible at the treasury.[1] But his reward was being offered the embassy at Constantinople, one not considered of vital importance by the establishment. A U.S. ambassador at

Constantinople had little to do but look after the interests of American missionaries in the empire and, on occasion, provide some assistance to insurance salespersons representing the big American companies, which were especially active there.

But events were to throw Morgenthau into a maze of activity that could not have been anticipated. His granddaughter, the distinguished historian Barbara Tuchman, has commented, "History broke over the Turkish capital, transforming it into one of the key diplomatic posts of the world. Morgenthau found himself in the role of the leading neutral ambassador, caretaker for the Allied embassies, protector and mediator for Christians, Jews, Armenians and every person and institution caught in the chaos of the Ottoman Empire."[2]

Morgenthau's commentary on these vital years provides a particularly penetrating view, not least because of his relative inexperience in the world of diplomacy. This meant that he did not pull his punches and remained active, alert, inquisitive, and purposeful. Because of his many years in business and the law, he could view events and personalities astutely and wisely.

Morgenthau makes no bones of the fact that all informed opinion was certain that at the time of the Allied attempt to get through the Dardanelles, the Young Turk regime was in its death throes. "Wangenheim and also nearly all of the German military and naval forces not only regarded the forcing of the Dardanelles as possible, but they believed it to be inevitable. . . . The weight of opinion, both lay and professional, inclined in favor of the allied fleets."[3]

In conversation with the mighty Talaat at this time, Morgenthau was told, "An attempt to force the Straits would succeed; it only depended on England's willingness to sacrifice a few ships." This, of course, was precisely what Churchill was saying in London during exactly the same period.

Another man at the U.S. embassy was Lewis Einstein. Because of his long years of service in Constantinople, he had been recalled there at the outbreak of war by Secretary of State William Jennings Bryan. Einstein confirmed Morganthau's view. Witty, urbane, and above all well-informed, he commented, "The bombardment of the entrance forts at the Dardanelles threw consternation into Turkey. The prospective fall of Constantinople was anticipated by both Germans and Turks, and every preparation was made for the immediate evacuation of the capital and the transfer of the seat of government to Eskisehir in the interior of Asia Minor." Further, he stated, "The credit of the Committee of Union and Progress which rules Turkey, was then at its lowest ebb, the treasury was empty, the country on the verge of ruin."[4]

To make the situation even more difficult, a gloomy reference in Liman's memoirs tells us of an outbreak of cholera among Turkish troops. His information came from reports he received from German military doctors throughout the empire. There was a total absence of medical resources to combat the outbreak.[5]

Military experts also expected Turkish defeat once the Allied fleet reached Constantinople. The military attaché at the Austrian embassy said, "The destruction of the outer forts of the Dardanelles and the repeated attempts at landing by the English and the French caused enormous excitement and literal panic. Not only the Turkish population but also the Government were scared of an imminent forcing of the Dardanelles by the enemy fleet and its appearance at the capital. The authorities consequently made all the preparations in anticipation of an evacuation of Constantinople. The Sultan's court, the Government and leading bureaucrats were to be transferred to Eskisehir; equipment, furniture, archives were sent there. The treasury, religious relics were all packed in great haste and sent to Konya. . . ." When, on March 18, 1915, "the news arrived in Constantinople that the entire Anglo-French fleet had penetrated the Dardanelles and had commenced the attack against the inner fortifications, a huge increase in activity could be seen in government circles and within the diplomatic corps. . . . Transports were commandeered on the Asiatic side, ships and special trains delegated for the Court, the ministries and the diplomatic corps. . . . There were obvious signs of an improved mood among the Greeks and Armenians of the city."[6]

What of the defenders of the forts, the Turkish and German gunners? They had acquitted themselves gloriously on the eighteenth of March and had pounded the Anglo-French fleet with everything at hand. But by the end of the day they had run out of ammunition. They knew the enemy fleet would reappear the next day. All logic pointed to it. A German journalist who spent some time with the gunners on that occasion was to write: "Dozens of German naval gunners who were manning the batteries of Chanakkale . . . told me later that they had quite made up their minds the fleet would ultimately win and that they themselves could not have held out much longer."[7]

But the Allied fleet did not reappear on the nineteenth of March. And when several days passed without sign of the enemy, the Turks were first amazed and then jubilant. The mighty British navy had been defeated! Here was Turkey, facing what was perceived as an invincible foe, bereft of ammunition, but nonetheless able to withstand the might of a British assault.

From lowly soldier to field general, a sense of pride began to communicate itself to all units of the Turkish army. On the twenty-fourth of March, six days after the frustrated Allied attack, Enver called Liman and asked him if he was prepared to take over command of the 5th Army, which was to be organized for the defense of the Dardanelles. Liman assented immediately. It was one of Enver's more intelligent decisions, as was Liman's subsequent one to enlist the services of an as yet relatively unknown colonel on his staff, Mustafa Kemal, who was to become the leader of modern Turkey.

All this made sound military sense.

It also created a breathing space in which the Young Turks, beneficiaries of the pusillanimity of the Entente strategists and of the shot in the arm this gave their regime, could put into effect their plans to eliminate an entire racial minority.

Chapter 7

Preamble
to a Genocide

In February 1915, while the British were hastily assembling their fleet off the island of Lemnos in the eastern Aegean Sea, a speech was being delivered at a closed session of the Central Committee of the Committee of Union and Progress. In it, the speaker expressed himself as follows:

> If we remain satisfied with the sort of local massacres which took place in Adana and elsewhere in 1909 . . . , if this purge is not general and final, it will inevitably lead to problems. Therefore it is absolutely necessary to eliminate the Armenian people in its entirety, so that there is no further Armenian on this earth and the very concept of Armenia is extinguished.
>
> We are now at war. We shall never have a more suitable opportunity than this. We need pay no attention to protests from the press or fear the intervention of the Powers. And

even if we were to pay attention, it will make no difference because it will be an accomplished fact for all time.

This time the action will produce total annihilation and it is essential that no single Armenian survives it. Perhaps there are those among you who feel it is bestial to go so far. You may ask, for instance, what harm can children, the elderly or the sick do to us that we feel compelled to work for their elimination. Or you may feel that only those guilty should be punished. . . .

I beg you, gentlemen, don't be weak. Control your feelings of pity. Otherwise these very feelings will bring about our own demise."[1]

These words were uttered by Dr. Nazim, who together with his medical colleague Dr. Behaeddin Shakir (whom we last met at the *Dashnak* conference in Erzurum in July 1914), were the leading executives of the genocide against the Armenians. "Both Nazim and Shakir," declares the leading authority on these men, "had received their medical education in Constantinople, with Nazim getting additional training in Paris, where, as political exiles, the two doctors were preparing the ground to overthrow the regime of Abdülhamīd. They helped precipitate the Young Turk revolution in 1908, and thereafter became permanent fixtures in the leadership of the Party. They achieved their positions of decisive power in the 1912–18 period, during which they exercised their authority behind the scenes (except for three months during which Dr. Nazim served as Minister of Education). During the post-revolutionary period, Dr. Nazim briefly served as Chief Physician at Saloniki Municipal Hospital, while Dr. Shakir was Professor of Legal (Ethical) Medicine at Constantinople Medical School."[2]

It is significant that the sentiments expressed by Nazim in his address to the Central Committee were repeated in a letter written some four years later by Adolf Hitler to a man named Gemlich. At the time, Hitler was acquiring a following as a public speaker in postwar Munich and as an authority on racism. He was also doing intelligence work for the army on left-wing political organizations that might provide a threat to public order. To Gemlich he wrote, "Anti-Semitism for purely emotional reasons will find its final expression in the form of pogroms. The anti-Semitism of reason, however, must lead to the systematic combating and elimination of Jewish privileges. Its ultimate goal must implacably be the total removal of the Jews."[3] In Germany, the Nazis would not trust the removal of the Jews to the vagaries of the occasional pogrom. It would have to be achieved surgically, and pity for the victim was a form of self-indulgence that could not be permitted.

Nazim's message was identical. Though the Young Turks were anticlerical, they were aided in their enterprise by the knowledge that the paramilitary formations they recruited (made up of brigands called *cetes*) were mainly extremist Muslims who would recall the injunction of the Sharia to treat the infidel as cattle. Armenian children could accordingly be dumped in the middle of the Black Sea and left to drown. (To a later generation of young Germans about to embark on wholesale murder, Nazi leader Heinrich Himmler was to comment that everybody knew one good Jew, but if one added up all the good Jews to be saved, there would be nobody left to eliminate.)

The high point of the Young Turk genocide of the Armenians, enunciated so devastatingly by Nazim and orchestrated by central direction from the Ministry of the Interior, can be placed in the time period of April to September 1915. But the killing started earlier, as demonstrated by March 20

New York Times reference to a whole plain strewn with Armenian bodies. In various areas of the wartime Ottoman Empire, individual commanders and individual military and paramilitary units, on their own initiative, raped and killed Armenians, drawing no fine distinctions between men, women, the aged, or children. The event reported by the *New York Times* was in fact perpetrated by the remnants of Enver's 3rd Army, aided by Kurds and brigands of all denominations. The entire plain of Alashgard, which before the war had been inhabited by some forty thousand Armenians, was totally devastated.[4] A similar devastation had been wrought in northeastern Persia by Khalil Bey in late 1914 when, in command of a force of twenty thousand regulars and ten thousand irregular Kurds, he let loose his men on Armenian and other Christian settlements there. Armenians who survived these attacks and still had some mobility tended to cross the nearest frontier, where they would wait for things to quiet down and then attempt to return to their homes—often with terrible results. In many cases, death awaited them. In a majority of cases, their homes had already been taken over by Kurds or Circassians or Muslims from other areas. A similar situation prevailed on the Turco-Russian frontier at the Caucasus. Survivors, refugees all, sought safety in Russia until Russian armies advanced in a southwesterly direction. Armenians anxious to retrieve their possessions in the *vilayets* they and their ancestors had called home for centuries often accompanied the advancing Russian armies, hoping the front line of battle would extend southwestward and the Turks would be to driven out.

The advancing Russian armies were indeed one of the few hopes for the beleaguered Armenians. A case in point is the Armenian settlement at the town of Van. Those who had stayed in Van remained under siege by Turkish forces. They believed that if only they could hold out until the Russian advance swept over the town, they might survive the nightmare. Armenians in Van therefore stayed in their quarter of the town and attempted to live through the blockade. While the Turkish siege continued, German consuls continued to send intelligence to Wangenheim about the misdeeds of Turkish units in their treatment of the indigenous Armenian population. On April 24, 1915, Wangenheim did something uncharacteristic. He had clearly been advised (possibly by the nearby German consul or by German officers serving near Van) that actions being taken against the Armenians there were particularly cruel. On this day he made his way to the Ministry of the Interior and demanded to see the minister, the powerful Talaat. Possibly urged on by German missionaries, Wangenheim wanted to stop the atrocities.

Talaat was unable to see him. Because April 24 was the day on which the intellectual and moral leadership of the entire Armenian community in Constantinople was rounded up to be assassinated, Talaat was otherwise occupied. Yes, there had been "disturbances" at Van, said a senior official with whom Wangenheim spoke. In reply, Wangenheim said that the German government hoped the Ottoman authorities would impose discipline locally so that these disturbances did not translate into an indiscriminate massacre of Armenians. In view of his later fence-sitting, these were strong words for Wangenheim.

On the same day, a report from Tiflis in Transcaucasia sent via Saint Petersburg and London to the *New York Times,* to be published next day, read as follows: "Refugees who have reached the Russian lines report that the massacre of Armenians by Mohammedans is being continued on an even greater scale. They say that all the inhabitants of ten villages near Van in Armenia have been put to death."

April 24 is now an important day on the Armenian calendar, a day set aside for remembrance.

It is also the day on which the reinforced Allied armada finally set sail for the Dardanelles, this time carrying a force of Australian, New Zealand, and British troops hastily trained and assembled in Egypt. The invasion, which ended ingloriously with Allied withdrawal some nine months later, is often called the Gallipoli campaign. It has been labeled the worst-prepared invasion in history. It has even been called "the coming of age of Australia." But it is also a sequel to those events on March 18, 1915, that arguably ushered in the death of the Armenian nation.

Chapter 8

THE YOUNG TURKS
AND THEIR IDEOLOGY

Before turning to the facts of the Young Turks' attempt to annihilate the Armenian nation, the question of motivation must be considered.

Were the Young Turks animated by an ideology, by a set of ideas?

By the time Turkey was involved in the First World War, its leaders were intent on cementing the Turkish hold on what they considered the irreducible minimum of Turkish territory. This was Anatolia, a region bordered by the Mediterranean on the west and the Caucasus mountains on the east. Within this area lay the ancient homeland of the Armenians. In eastern Anatolia were the settlements of the large Armenian plateau, while in western Anatolia, bordering the Mediterranean, was the old Armenian kingdom of Cilicia. Because Turkish claims to the area were based on conquest, a set of ideas was needed to justify Turkey's continued hegemony there. This need led the adoption of *Turanism,* which stressed the great qualities of the Turks and gave credence to the new racial ideas with which the Young Turks had replaced the multiethnic nature of Ottomanism. It provided the intellectual *raison d'être* for the new vision of Turkey so beloved of Enver and the other leading lights among the Young Turks.

When the Young Turks came into power, they were confronted with a governmental bureaucracy that in large part relied on graft and nepotism. They not only had to change the system fundamentally, but they had to offer to the mass of Turks some form of mobility and some form of patriotism that might inspire them to introduce basic changes. (This theme would be taken up more radically by the successor to the Young Turks, Mustafa Kemal.)

The origin of Turanism, which the Young Turks adopted, developed in the nineteenth century. It was in Hungary that the first Turanian society was founded by a Hungarian named Alois von Paikert. The first obstacle the believers in Turanism had to overcome was the widespread view of Turks as coarse and uneducated.[1]

This was not a view held only by foreigners. Within the Ottoman Empire itself, the vast mass of Turkish peasantry was—with some reason—considered by the upper classes to be totally unenlightened. At the end of the nineteenth century, a group of educated Turks were invited by a foreign scholar named Hermann Vambery to state what qualities they believed they had in common with the Turkic tribes of central Asia. Their reactions were utterly negative. For them, the very notion of *Turk* carried with it a picture of coarseness, lack of sophistication, and ignorance.

To establish the concept of Turanism, Paikert and his followers had to go backward in time to the centuries of Turkish conquest, to the recapitulation and glorification of those qualities that had enabled their ancestors, who had started out from central Asia, to overrun everything in their way. They had to rediscover the roots of Turkish pride, which had become severely damaged for two or three centuries.

Even at the height of Ottoman power in the fourteenth, fifteenth, and sixteenth centuries, the rational, highly organized, and highly efficient bureaucracy of the empire had been made up of Christians absorbed by conquest, not of native Turks. A leading historian of the Ottomans has observed, "Whether captured in battle, recruited through drafts, purchased in the market, presented as gifts to the Sultan, or enlisting voluntarily in his service, Christians accepted conversion to Islam, celibacy, separation from their families, and renunciation of all property. For this their reward was a comprehensive course of education and training on Spartan lines, in the Palace School for pages. This led to a discerning selection for that career in public service best suited to their talents, with opportunities for promotion to the highest offices of state. It meant in effect rule through the conquered in the interests of the conqueror. Unnatural as such enslavement might appear in the eyes of the West, it proved in its own context to be an enlightened and practical formula for using in full the qualities and skills of the Sultan's young Christian subjects, to the benefit of the Empire and indeed of the slaves themselves."[2]

Paikert advanced the claim that no fewer than 600 million people across vast areas of Asia and Europe were Turkic in origin. He included those people speaking languages of Finno-Ugrian derivation, which were held to be Turkic. Since the ancestors of the Ottomans had been essentially nomadic and thus widespread, it was possible for Paikert to argue that a monumental future would result from an association of all their descendants.

This is of course hyperbole. But it had an effect on at least one of the leaders of the Young Turks. The heroic future that Enver believed must be his depended on the realization of a vast enterprise in which all these people of Turkic origin might be united. It was this certainty that kept the young patriot's eyes firmly fixed on Transcaucasia. He was certain that a Turkish patriot must cross the great mountain ranges of the Caucasus to unite the Turkic peoples. Among the Azerbaijanis, who were Turkey's northeastern neighbors, Enver and his associates indeed found a very warm response, for Azerbaijanis were desperate to throw off the Russian yoke and combine with members of their own racial family. But when Enver and the Young Turks looked to the southern and western reaches of the once-great empire they had inherited, all they saw was irredentism. The Arabs situated there clearly wanted their independence, and the Turkish army had to maintain large forces in southern Arabia just to keep the Yemenis at bay. Turkey's future, as the Young Turks saw it, lay across the Caucasus—to a large degree because they were not wanted in north Africa or Arabia.

But something stood in the way—Armenia, historical Armenia. It straddled the line of putative Turkish advance in the direction the Young Turks wished to move. What was more, the Armenians were constantly in touch with Russia, Turkey's longtime enemy. Added to this were the facts that a large amount of trade was in Armenian hands and that Armenians were generally better educated, more industrious, and more literate than the Turks. It is from such rifts in status and cultural background that great antipathies grow.

And so the Young Turks preached that the Turkish peasant must be glorified. What other source was there for a Turkish renewal? A virtue had to be made of the peasant's lack of sophistication. To the Young Turks, the disgust with which the more cultured Turks of Constantinople viewed the Turkic peoples of central Asia was a cynical abandonment of all that was valuable in Turkey. "Fatherland for the Turks is neither Turkey nor Turkestan," so the Young Turks' spokesperson Ziya Goeckalp wrote in a famous poem, "Their fatherland is a great and eternal land, Turan." Thus Turanism was adopted.

Turanism certainly did not fill thousands of books, as did the literature the Nazis provided as the ideological background for the new Germany. But this is to compare two vastly different societies. What they had in common was a sadistic relentlessness in pursuit of their prey. The starting point for the Young Turks was the need to cleanse Anatolia of foreign influence. This might then be used as a jumping off point for excursions in the direction of central Asia. Eliminating Armenians was, so they thought, an essential part of this design. It might, therefore, be argued that the chief victims of Turanism were the Armenians.

Chapter 9

GENOCIDE

Things which we find scarcely credible excite little surprise in Turkey.

—Viscount James Bryce, House of Lords, October 6, 1915

This oft-quoted comment from the onetime British ambassador to the United States had its origin in the level of cruelty witnessed in Turkey by countless foreigners. Those with an appreciation of history knew that severing an opponent's head, impaling it on a stick, and brandishing it about was a practice indulged in by the Christian knights during the Crusades. Some six hundred years after the last of the Crusades, the legions of photographs that commemorated the genocide against the Armenians included those showing Turkish soldiers posing next to a pile of Armenian skulls. It was difficult for Westerners to absorb that this was happening in the twentieth century.

Certainly, the reputation of the Turks for cruelty had been established, and even preserved in a simile: as cruel as a Turk. The cruelty evinced by Turkish army units in their attempt during 1876 to suppress independence efforts among the Bulgarians had shocked Europe. An elderly and infirm former prime minister of England, William Gladstone, left his sickbed to fulminate in public against the Turks when, during those campaigns, the first news of Turkish acts of cruelty were published in the British press. For a hundred years and more, Europe had been nurtured on the notion of the inevitability of human progress. Turkey, it seemed, was taking the world back to the Dark Ages.

Once the Young Turks decided to annihilate the Armenians, there remained the question of what form this annihilation should take. Clearly the absence of a developed industry within the empire made it impossible to create what could be called a Turkish Auschwitz. The form eventually taken by the death mills of Auschwitz was the result of continuous experimentation by German engineers entrusted with the task of creating a superefficient machine for the destruction and disposal of human beings. But the executives of this genocide had at their disposal the most sophisticated railway network in Europe. The transport of the victims to the point of disposal was relatively simple; they were packed in railway carriages and, in accordance with well-coordinated plans, transferred to their place of oblivion. Of course, before graduating to these highly efficient methods of disposal, the Germans had experimented with mass shootings behind the lines of their army's advance. They had recruited their *Einsatzgruppen* (SS assault squads) for this purpose. But the sheer quantity of humans they wished to extinguish militated against continuing in this fashion. A more streamlined method had to be developed.

The Young Turks had no railroad system to collect and dispose of the Armenians. Despite the efforts to proceed with the construction of the Berlin-to-Baghdad railroad, there were few miles of track available, and the condition of most highways was appalling. Consequently, those charged by the *Teshkilati Mahsusa* with the responsibility of eliminating the Armenian community evolved a system of such primitive brutality that even today, after our century has witnessed the indiscriminate massacre of many millions, the *Ittihadist* project still evokes the most fundamental feelings of revulsion. There is no doubt that if a more sophisticated machinery for slaughter had been available, the Young Turks would have used it. Lacking such machinery, their system of eradication worked along the following lines, as described by one scholar of the period:

> Initially all the able-bodied men of a certain town or village would be ordered, either by a public crier or by an official proclamation nailed to the walls, to present themselves at the *konak* [government building]. The proclamation stated that the Armenian population would be deported, gave the official reasons for it, and assured them that the government was benevolent. Once at the *konak*, they would be jailed for a day or two. No reason was given. Then they would be led out of jail and marched out of town. At the first lonely halting place they would be shot, or bayoneted to death. Some days later the old men and the women and children were summoned in the same way; they were often given a few days grace, but then they had to leave. It was their misfortune not to be killed at the first desolate place. The government's reasoning appears to have been: the men might pose a threat—leaders might spring up among them, who would defy the order; but why waste valuable lead on women, old men and children? Instead they were forced to walk, endlessly, along pre-arranged routes, until they died from thirst, hunger, exposure or exhaustion. Most were driven south to the burning Syrian desert; a few from Cilicia were initially sent in a north-westerly direction,

towards the marshlands of Konya and the gloomy, empty landscape around the great salt lake. All suffered atrociously as convoy after convoy, accompanied by gendarmes, was moved on. . . . If they stopped, exhausted, they were mercilessly whipped by the Turkish soldiers [some regular, some irregular] until they continued.[1]

The Turkish escort troops described in this passage were a motley of different formations. To a large degree they had been recruited by Behaeddin Shakir; many were *cetes* recently released from the jails for the express purpose of butchering Armenians. Their training and their disposition was in the hands of Shakir, who in the winter of 1914–1915 was seen repeatedly in the Armenian *vilayets*, laying the groundwork for the project.

Despite the increasing political activity in the Armenian communities since the 1880s, there were only a few who guessed that a government-led directive in February 1915 to relocate the Armenians away from battle areas meant, in reality, annihilation. In any event, what should hundreds of thousands of these innocent victims know about higher policy?

There were, however, some survivors, and from them we can reconstruct what happened. Some of them responded to British and French requests after the war to supply statements that might be used as evidence in court against any alleged war criminals. Such a person was Pailadzu Captanian, widow of Arakel Captanian of Samsun. She deposed the following under oath at the office of the British high commission in Constantinople on three occasions between January 15 and February 2, 1920:

I am the daughter of the late Noghos Torikian, merchant of Merzifun. I married in 1908 and lived chiefly in Samsun.

About 20 June 1915 in pursuance of orders received from Constantinople and transmitted to the Armenian population by posters we were ordered to be deported. Nedjami Bey was then *vali* [governor] of Samsun. I left my two boys in the charge of the Greek Metropolitan. My husband and I travelled fifteen days together on the road to Tokat via Amarsia. Arrived in Tunus, two hours from Chiflik in the *vilayet* of Sivas, the escort separated all the men and locked them up in a stable, about 300, all pressed together. I was permitted to say goodbye to my husband through a window. Not one of these 300 is alive today. We, the women, were pushed on the road to Malatia, avoiding Sivas. The next day we heard all had been killed. Muammer was *vali* of Sivas and the order came through him; the actual butchers I do not know. The escort and the chief of escort were continually changing.

One day's march from Tunus we were all stopped by the escort and robbed of all our jewels, valuables and money. This was done systematically. It took a day and a night. Many women saved some gold liras by swallowing them. I gave up my jewels and a gold lira, all the rest I possessed, 9 liras I saved in a horse's nosebag. We were one month on the road from Samsun to Malatia, avoiding Sivas. It is impossible to say how many Armenians left Samsun and how many arrived at Malatia, for the numbers—apart from murders and deaths from starvation etc.—were continually changing.

We passed Kangal (SSE of Sivas) and arrived at Hassan Chelebi on the main road from Sivas to Malatia, a small village in the Harput *vilayet*. Here the men were again separated from the women, locked up and later led out of the village and massacred. I was in the village at the time and saw the men led out of the village towards a deep valley. They were escorted by gendarmes and followed by the

Turks of the village, all armed with swords, knives and sticks. This was in the early afternoon. Before nightfall the Turkish butchers returned carrying the clothing of the slaughtered Armenian men. I estimate their number as over 400, chiefly from Amassia. Some of the Samsun lads who were not murdered at Tunus were murdered here.

A week later I reached Malatia. We did not go into the town itself. Here those who still had horses were deprived of them. By leaving my group at night and sheltering with a newly arrived one I managed to remain in the open near Malatia for some days. . . . At last I left Malatia and went on southwards. It took us about six weeks to reach the river (100 kilometres). We were sent up and down mountains, never on a road. The escorts were trying to kill us by hunger and exhaustion. All this rough country was full of corpses; the stench was terrible. Of the group with which I left Malatia, certainly more than a half perished before reaching the Euphrates. . . . The crossing of the Euphrates was a terrible performance, in the barges the boatmen set upon us, beat us and robbed us again, nearing the bank they threw us into the water and many were drowned.[2]

Note the comment about the corpses. By December 1915, there were thousands of them all over the countryside. The news reached Talaat at the Ministry of the Interior. He sent a round-robin to all *valis* by coded cable on December 19 of that year, instructing them as follows: "I have been advised that in certain areas unburied corpses are still to be seen. I ask you to issue the strictest instructions so that the corpses and their debris in your *vilayet* are buried. Henceforth any officials in *kazas* [subdistricts] in which corpses are found will be dismissed, their names having been communicated to me."[3]

This was not the first time the issue of unburied corpses had been raised at the ministry and at the offices of local *valis*.

Talaat Pasha, the leading political brain among the Young Turk leaders. (AKG Photo)

By September 1915, the risk of disease (and, of course, the subsidiary aesthetic problem) was beginning to alarm the authorities. On the nineteenth of that month a cable signed by Sabit Bey, *vali* of Mamuret-ul-Aziz, read as follows: "Contrary to my repeated instructions I am told there is still far too large a number of corpses along the roads. It is surely superfluous to refer again to the obvious consequences of this. The Minister has just ordered severe punishment to those officials who are guilty of negligence in this matter. I repeat once again: send a sufficient number of gendarmes to all sections of the *vilayet* with the duty of burying all corpses not yet interred, within the eyesight of appropriate officials, and confirm back to me."[4]

At the Ministry of the Interior, Talaat had been confident that Shakir would be able to recruit the sadistic types entrusted with the on-the-spot murder of the Armenians. However, these worthies had obviously shown little appetite for burying the corpses. An abundance of telegrams from Sabit during the awful months of 1915 have found their way into the British Public Records Office. Sabit clearly wanted to create the right impression with his superiors. In a cable dated July 28, 1915, we find him advising Talaat, "The first company from Erzurum was received at Kuru Chai by the temporary *kaimakam* [commissioner] of Equina, Abdulkader Effendi, who accompanied it, safe and sound, with the *kaimakam* of Kemach as far as Equina. . . . Measures have been taken to ensure the passage of the second and third convoys in similar conditions. I have also requested the *mutassarif* [governor] of Malatia to place all convoys arriving in that town under the protection of safe *kaimakams* and officers."[5]

Note the reference to the second and third convoys. This is evidence of forward planning and shows how threadbare are the subsequent Turkish claims that the treatment of the Armenians was a spontaneous result of the passions of local Turkish communities. There is nothing spontaneous about the work of Sabit; indeed, he is obviously currying favor with his superiors at the ministry. But if Sabit's motive was to demonstrate his efficiency and reliability, he clearly failed because little progress was made in disposing of the corpses. On September 10, 1915, he was obliged to complain to a Reshid, *mutassarif* of Malatia: "In Husnimanssur and Behesni I have been told there are corpses in a state of decomposition. In previous and recent communications I have repeatedly said that this will not be allowed either from the political viewpoint of the government or from the perspective of public health. . . . Please give the most unambiguous instructions to the *kaimakams* of the *kazas* mentioned to bury all corpses."[6]

By late 1915 it was clear that the centrally administered genocide had become visible throughout the empire. Although the Young Turk leaders had chosen a wartime period to eliminate the Armenians, they would have preferred to keep the details away from the prying and critical eyes of foreigners. One wonders how this could possibly have been achieved; nonetheless, Talaat occasionally attempted to redress the situation. He sent a number of messages, especially to the administration of the city of Aleppo, that demonstrate this:

> From interventions which have recently been made by the American Ambassador at Constantinople,[7] on behalf of his government, it appears that American consuls are obtaining information by secret means. In spite of our assurances that the Armenian deportations will be accomplished in safety and comfort, they remain unconvinced. From the point of view of the present policy it is most important that foreigners who are in those areas, are persuaded that the expulsion of the Armenians is in truth only deportation. For this reason it is important that for the sake of appearances, a show of gentle dealing shall be made for a time and the usual measures be taken in suitable places. It is recommended that those people who have given such information be arrested and handed over to the military authorities for trial by court martial.[8]

There was not the slightest doubt abroad that the Armenians were being decimated. After all, the Allied powers had sent a warning to the Young Turks as early as May 24, 1915, that they would pursue the guilty.

At Aleppo there must have been some doubt among the members of the city council about the specifics of Talaat's orders. The minister had already advised them on September 3, 1915, "We recommend that the operations which we have ordered you to undertake shall first be carried out on the men of the said people [the Armenians] and that you subject the women and children to them also. Appoint reliable officials for this." On December 11 Talaat sent another coded telegram to Aleppo: "We hear that correspondents of certain Armenian newspapers travelling in those parts have faked some letters and a photograph showing certain criminal actions, which they have given to the American consuls. Arrest and destroy such persons."

There must, however, have been some officials working in the city government of Aleppo who were still unable to comprehend the severity of the *Ittihadist* measures. Did Talaat mean to annihilate the children, too? On September 21 he cabled them: "There is no need for an orphanage. It is not the time to give way to sentiment and feed the orphans, prolonging their lives. Send them away to the desert and confirm back to us."

Yet on the twenty-third of January 1916, a by now somewhat irritated Talaat was forced to cable Aleppo: "At a time when there are thousands of Moslem refugees and the widows of our martyrs [Turks fallen in the war] are in need of food and protection, it is not expedient to incur extra expense by feeding the children left by Armenians. It is necessary for these children to be turned out of your *vilayet* and sent with the caravans to the places of deportation. Those that have been kept until now are also to be sent away, in compliance with our previous orders."[9]

Aleppo was on the way to a massive staging area in the Syrian desert at which sometimes thousands and thousands of starving, emaciated, and disease-ridden Armenians could be seen simply awaiting death. The instruction from Talaat that children should be sent to "places of deportation" meant consigning them to death in the Syrian Desert.

A project as huge as the genocide against the Armenians involved the mobilization of thousands of public servants, police officials, and army and paramilitary units, together with the *cetes* who acted as escorts and murderers. Yet there were some brave Turks who managed to defy the orders—brave because defiance normally earned them a death sentence. An example of this rare breed was Shefik Bey, who, in a deposition at the British high commission on September 16, 1920, testified as follows:

> I myself in April 1915 was *kaimakam* of Chavas in the *vilayet* of Van near Urmia. Because I was known to the *vali* Djevdet as lenient to the Armenians, I was sent on 5 April 1915 to Anatolia in Mosul *vilayet* to settle a quarrel between two Kurd tribes. I returned to Chavas on 12 May and found that nearly all the Armenians of the *kaza* had been massacred by order of Halil Bey (later Pasha) who had remained some four days in the *kaza* on his way back from his expedition to Urumia and Balmas. At this time Babri Bey was Halil's Chief of Staff, Bekir Sami Bey was in command of the cavalry and Aralan Bey was in command of the Irregulars. Thus these four must of necessity be held responsible for the massacres. In my *kaza* there were twenty Christian villages, in Diza there were between six hundred and seven hundred Christians. On my return after five weeks' absence there were left not more than a total of two thousand five hundred Christian females with no men at all. They had been massacred on the spot and had not been deported. The population was wiped out by the regular Turkish cavalry,

the Turkish Irregulars and the Kurds. Between Diza and Mush the same thing happened. . . .

In my *kaza* the Christian population were peaceable folk, they had supplied all the transport and provisions that I had ordered. To my knowledge they had not engaged in any insurrectionary movement, they had not gone over to the Russians and I knew of no treason among them. There were no Christian intellectuals in my *kaza,* there were not even any schools. Few spoke their own racial language. . . .

The reason for the massacre was merely the carrying out of the Panturanian policy of the Committee of Union and Progress, as explained to me by Omar Nadji, now dead, the chief CUP delegate to the eastern *vilayets* in September 1914. He was in his cups [drunk] at the time and he knew that I was against the Committee.

On the Russian advance I was appointed *kaimakam* of Shemdinan. . . . This transfer took place in June, 1915. I remained there about a year as *kaimakam* and acting *mutassarif* of Hakkiari. When I arrived at Chandinan the Christian population had already been despoiled. The remaining refugees were in Urumia. The 200 families of Christians and Jews that I had saved in Chevas I took with me to Shendinan. These and about 200 further Christian families that I found in Shendinan I took with me to Akra in the *vilayet* of Mosul, whence I fled in May 1916 before the Russian advance. I left the approximately 400 families in this *kaza* in the care of the *kaimakam* Fakhri Bey. Then I went to Mosul and returned shortly afterwards to Akra as acting *kaimakam.* Here I found the Christian families (my refugees) all well. . . . [Shefik Bey goes on to describe a number of further appointments he held until his final posting as *kaimakam* of Bulanik, where he resigned because] the town and villages were destroyed, there were no resident inhabitants left, only brigands; there was no administration and even my own personal property and official books and papers were taken from me.[10]

It may be argued that the testimony of a man who held so many posts within the *Ittihadist* regime while claiming to be its avowed enemy must be questionable. However, his translator (who translated the deposition from Turkish into French) was an Armenian called Boyadjian, whom the British had found trustworthy and who was unlikely to have been a friend of anyone in the Young Turk regime. Furthermore, a large number of the Christians Shefik Bey claims to have saved from annihilation were Nestorians (Syrian Christians), but this is splitting hairs, for once the Turks were on the rampage, they drew no fine distinctions—an infidel was an infidel.

A very important point to note is Shefik's statement that the Christians in his *kaza* "had not been engaged in any insurrectionary movement, had not gone over to the Russians and I knew of no treason among them." As noted earlier, it has been the consistent claim of the Turkish establishment for over eighty years that what happened to the Armenians during the First World War resulted from their complicity in a vast conspiracy. In any event, one might ask what role the obviously nonpolitical elements in a population—women, children, the aged, and the infirm—would play in such a conspiracy, real or imagined.

Nonetheless, to buttress these claims, Turkish apologists are wont to produce photographs showing piles of small arms forcibly obtained from Armenians bent on destroying the Ottoman Empire. The circumstances under which these arms were gathered is another chapter in itself. From the fall of 1914 onward, all Armenians were required to surrender any arms in their possession to the authorities. To accomplish this, units of

Turkish regular and irregular troops made their rounds of the Armenian settlements. If no arms were produced, the Turks had recourse to bastinado: beating the soles of the alleged miscreant's feet while his body hung upside down, until the feet were no longer usable and amputation could not be avoided. Many Armenians thought it was the lesser of two evils to purchase a rifle from a Muslim neighbor (at a grossly inflated price) and hand it over. When piles of these arms had been collected, they were carefully photographed and stored away as "proof" of the insurrectionary tendencies of the Armenians, who, in any event, had been given the right to bear arms only since the revolution of 1908.

The impossibility of keeping the facts of the genocide away from the eyes of foreigners is nowhere more amply demonstrated than in the series of reports the American ambassador received from his consuls throughout the empire. In this regard, the U.S. consulate at Aleppo was particularly busy. In its report to Morgenthau dated April 21, 1915, the consulate enclosed a summary of local conditions described by the Reverend John E. Merrill, president of Central Turkey College at Aintab (now Gaziantep):

> Deportation of families is only another form of accomplishing the object of massacre, to destroy the influence and power of the Christian population. The outraging of women, the separation of families, confiscation of property and personal insult are fit subject for the indignation of those who look on but are powerless to interfere, and for the interference of those who can. The crushing and deportation of the educated and able Christian population of the Marash field is a direct blow at American missionary in-

terests, menacing the results of more than fifty years of work and many thousands of dollars of expenditure. The missionaries in Marash have been given absolute guarantees by the Turkish military authorities of their personal safety, but are obliged to watch the execution of orders which threaten to remove the churches and institutions which have been brought into being all through their field. . . . If we believed that those men and women and children were guilty of treasonable conduct we would be the first to acquiesce in righteous punishment. Believing that the number of those worthy of punishment is exceedingly limited, we cannot but view the situation with the greatest concern.[11]

On May 12, 1915, J. B. Jackson, the U.S. consul at Aleppo, advised Morgenthau as follows:

Between 4,300 and 4,500 families, about 28,000 persons, are being removed by order of the Government from the districts of Zeitoun and Marash to distant places where they are unknown, and in distinctly non-Christian communities. Thousands have already been sent to the northwest into the provinces of Konia [Konya], Cesaria, Castamouni, etc., while others have been taken southeasterly as far as Deir-el-Zor, and reports say, to the vicinity of Baghdad. The misery these people are suffering is terrible to imagine. To go into detail would be a useless waste of time, for all the sufferings that a great community would be subject to in such circumstances are being experienced. Their property they are unable to sell as they are given but a few hours to prepare for the journey, and the Government is installing Mohammedan families in their homes, and who take possession of everything as soon as the Armenians have departed. Rich and poor alike, Protestant, Gregorian, Orthodox and

Catholic, are all subject to the same order. The local pastors and priests and their flocks, without distinction. The old, middle aged, young, the strong and the sick, being driven in herds to the four points of the compass to a fate which none can predict. Few are permitted the opportunity of riding except occasionally on an ox or a donkey, the sick drop by the wayside, women in critical condition giving birth to children, that according to reports, many mothers strangle or drown because of the lack of means to care for. Fathers exiled in one direction, mothers in another, the young girls and small children in yet another. According to reports from reliable sources the accompanying gendarmes are told that they may do as they wish with the women and girls. The writer has seen personally several parties of the men that passed through Aleppo, and who were in the most deplorable plight, and wonders what must have been the condition of the others that naturally were much less able to resist such treatment.

In Marash alone there are 6 Gregorian Orthodox Armenian churches, 1 Armenian Congregational, 1 Armenian Catholic and 1 Latin Catholic church, about 12 Armenian schools, 1 American, 1 German school, 1 American girls' orphanage, 1 German orphanage and a German hospital, practically all of which will be left without congregation or attendance. . . .

The Armenians themselves say that they would by far have preferred a massacre, which would have been less disastrous to them.[12]

Henry Morgenthau, a deeply compassionate man and an irrepressible activist, made repeated visits to Talaat at the Ministry of the Interior and used every avenue open to him to ameliorate the lot of the Armenians. But even he was accused of racism. As a result of pressure placed on him by the Jewish community in the United States, Morgenthau was asked to rescue a few thousand penniless and Orthodox Jews who had left Russia for Palestine (to escape pogroms and live out their declining years in the Holy Land) and now found themselves considered enemy aliens by the Ottoman authorities; they were, after all, considered Russians. Morgenthau, a Jew but not a Zionist, managed to arrange the escape of these impoverished and elderly exiles—a U.S. ship took them aboard off the coast of Palestine and transferred them to Egypt. It was from Egypt that the correspondent of the *London Times* (whom we shall meet again in another context) chastised Morgenthau. If only, opined this journalist, Morgenthau had not spent so much time looking after his coreligionists, he might have been able to rescue a few more Armenians. This is a particularly insidious comment about Morgenthau, who could not have done more than he did to try to persuade Talaat to abandon the program against the Armenians. At one point, Talaat was sufficiently intrigued to ask him why he, a Jew, was making so great an effort on behalf of Christians. This, and the attitude of the *London Times* correspondent, simply demonstrate the tunnel vision symptomatic of the age, a blinkered view of history that was enlisted, as we shall shortly see, in the evaluation of the conduct of Germans in the Ottoman Empire during the war.

The empire was full of foreigners who needed only eyes to see the decimation of the Armenians. There were plenty of sources and routes for the information to reach the Allied powers. Refugees who had reached the Russian border, ordinary travelers who made their way to Greece, all were able to keep the West informed. On the twenty-fourth of May 1915, the

Young Turk regime was warned by England, France, and Russia in a public statement to the press of that day: "The Allied Governments announce publicly to the Sublime Porte that they will hold all the members of the Ottoman Government as well as such of their agents as are implicated, personally responsible for such massacres." The entire non-Turkish world, therefore, was aware of the fate of the Armenians.

There have been some strange opinions about the timing of the genocide. One historian has expressed the view that the genocide took place only because the Turks were unable to achieve a genuine military victory and therefore let loose their fury on unarmed civilians: "The Turks discovered the relatively facile joys of slaughtering enemy civilians, however irrelevant, or even domestic scapegoats, in preference to the heavy sacrifices of their own soldiers in rational campaigns leading to a bona fide military victory. In fact it was during the campaign in the Dardanelles that at the expense of the Armenians the Turks pioneered the revival of genocide as a popular modern compensation for military impotence."[13]

This is a strange verdict for a variety of reasons. The genocide did not go into top gear until the Turks were conducting a spectacularly able defense of the Gallipoli Peninsula against a (for those times) large invasion fleet. In addition, it misses the whole point of a genocide to suggest that it takes place as a kind of soft option. All genocides have in common a contempt for rational military and economic thinking. Their practitioners are normally carried away by concepts of race and nation. They do not care about the diversion of soldiers or material that might otherwise serve the purposes of victory. If Hitler, for example, had enlisted the Jews in the German cause, he would have had some of the most patriotic and able elements of the population on his side. In Turkey there was a continuous battle between the *Ittihadist* higher-ups and the German engineers sent to continue the construction of the Berlin-to-Baghdad railroad. The Turks wanted the Germans to surrender the Armenian workers to their program of genocide. The Germans maintained that without the skills offered by the Armenian workers, the construction of the vital line would come to a standstill. The Germans accordingly went to considerable lengths to hide their Armenian workers from the *Ittihadist* inspectors.

One Armenian historian has argued that the direct motivation for the genocide is not clear: "The question still remains unanswered today whether it was the Turkish defeat at Sarikamish which is responsible for the decision of the leaders of the Young Turks to arrange the physical annihilation of the Armenian people, or on the other hand the Turkish victory in the Dardanelles campaign of 18 March 1915 which produced the changeover from a form of national consciousness to a type of brutal chauvinism."[14]

It must surely be arguable that the leading lights on the Special Committee of the Committee of Union and Progress had decided well before the retreat from Sarikamish or the victory at the Dardanelles to annihilate the Armenians. The sources for the genocide are multiple. The Hamidian massacres of the 1890s, those of Cilicia in 1909, and the intermittent but continuous persecution of Armenians in between these events suggest a current—persistent and vengeful—against the Armenians. The existence of Armenian volunteers in the Russian army simply gave an added boost to forces already poisoning Turkish attitudes, bringing to a boil a cauldron that had been stewing for decades. And behind the actions of the Young Turks was the continuous and insidious presence of Turanism, which preached the elimination of the Armenians.

Almost as an afterthought, and possibly as a reaction to the Allied declaration of May 24, 1915, a cloak of legality was provided for the initiative on May 27 (by which time the genocide was well under way) in the form of a Provisional Law for the Deportation of Persons under Suspicion of Espionage. Article 2 of this law stated: "Army commanders, corps and division commanders may, if military necessity so dictates, transfer any person or persons suspected of espionage, to other areas for purposes of resettlement."

Surely there is no real doubt as to what this transfer of persons, or deportation, meant. The chief of the *Teshkilati Mahsusa*, Behaeddin Shakir, sent a coded telegram on June 21, 1915, to Sabit Bey, *vali* of Mamuret-ul-Aziz, in which he asked, "Are your area's deported Armenians being liquidated? Are the dangerous people you mentioned being destroyed? Or are they being merely deported and exiled? Clarify this point, my brother."[15]

The telling word in this communication is "merely." Armenian victims were not simply being moved to areas far away from those in which the war was being fought. They were, to use the language of Shakir, being liquidated.

It was not only the English-speaking press that expressed its horror at what was taking place in the wartime Ottoman Empire. In the Roman newspaper *Il Messagero* on August 25, 1915, the erstwhile Italian consul at Trebizond gave the following description of what he had seen:

> The passing of the gangs of Armenian exiles beneath the windows and before the door of the Consulate; their

prayers for help, when neither I nor any other could do anything to answer them; the city in a state of siege, guarded at every point by 15,000 troops in complete war equipment, by thousands of police agents, by bands of volunteers and by the members of the Committee of Union and Progress; the lamentations, the tears, the abandonments, the imprecations, the many suicides, the instantaneous deaths from sheer terror, the sudden unhinging of men's reason, the conflagrations, the shooting of victims in the city; the ruthless searches through houses and in the countryside; the hundreds of corpses found every day along the exile road . . . the children torn away from their families or from the Christian schools, and handed over by force to Moslem families, or else placed by hundreds on board ship in nothing but their shirts, and then capsized and drowned in the Black Sea and the River Deyirmen Dere— these are my last ineffaceable memories of Trebizond, memories which still, at a months' distance, torment my soul and almost drive me frantic.[16]

Captain Harry Armstrong, the ranking officer among a group of British prisoners being force-marched through the Mesopotamian desert by a Turkish army unit, remembered his first meeting with Armenians in the following way: "I asked permission to get a drink from a nearby spring. It bubbled and laughed its way out of a cave between two trees. The water came out foul, for the cave was full of dead bodies."[17]

Because of the devoted and punctilious work of the German pastor Johannes Lepsius, it has been possible to reconstruct the approximate schedule set up by the *Ittihadists* for the extermination of the Armenians. By following the messages sent from outlying German consulates to the German embassy in Constantinople, Lepsius was able to create a table showing the roundups that took place in each *vilayet.* These are his findings:

Date (in 1915)	Place
June 14–July 15	From Erzurum
June 24	From Shabin-Karahissar
June 25	From Mamuret-ul-Aziz
June 26	From Sivas
June 26	From Trebizond
June 26	From Samsun
June 27	From Erzurum (again)
July 1	Massacre at Bitlis
July 10	Massacre at Mush
July 15	Massacre at Malatia
July 27	Deportations from the coastal region of Cilicia and Antioch
July 28	From Aintab (now Gaziantep), Killis, and Adiaman
July 30	From Suedije
August 12–19	Deportations from western Anatolia (Ismid, Brusa, Adabasar, etc.)
August 16	From Marash
August 16	From Konya
August 19	Massacre in Urfa[18]

Lepsius compiled his table using German sources. Because they were a very pronounced presence in the Ottoman Empire during this entire period, the actions of Germans have produced some very heated disputes. They were, after all, the allies of the Turks. Did they aid and abet their allies in the execution of their program? Did they do enough to attempt to stop it? These are questions that we shall address in the next chapter.

Chapter 10

GERMANS AND TURKS, GERMANS AND ARMENIANS

"**M**ilitarily Turkey amounts to nothing! Reports from our military mission provide no comfort whatsoever. The army is in a state which defies description. It is lifeless, beyond redemption, in a state of agony. Our military mission is like the officials of some medical faculty around the death-bed of a dying patient."[1]

These were not the evaluations of some junior member of Liman's staff. They were uttered just over three months before the outbreak of the First World War by Colonel General Helmuth Johannes Ludwig von Moltke. He was in a privileged position to know the truth of the situation; at the time, he was chief of the German general staff. Two months later, while at Carlsbad, he confided to his Austrian colleague Conrad von Hoetzendorf, "The Turkish army is absolutely worthless. It has no weapons, no munitions, no clothes. The officers' wives go begging on the street."[2]

Even Emperor William II himself, on whose initiative the German approach to Turkey had rested, was forced to admit just before the outbreak of war, "News about the Turkish army, communicated to me in all secrecy, describes the situation as hopeless . . . there is a huge number of epidemics and corpses, more than two thousand infected at Adrianopolis, including sixty cases of cholera."[3]

None of the German brass, therefore, were under any illusions about the state of Turkish arms. But the emperor tended to view the army as his personal plaything, so it made little sense for the German officers to emphasize their forebodings too noisily. In any event, if Germany sat at Constantinople, it could prevent Allied access to Russia via the Straits and the Black Sea; this was more of a factor than the value or otherwise of the Turkish army. And there were substantial economic reasons for maintaining a strong presence there. As we have seen, large investments had already been made in the Berlin-to-Baghdad railway.

Like Liman von Sanders, all the Germans stationed in the Ottoman Empire had learned quickly that things were different in Turkey. A new verb had been coined by junior German officers; any colleague who had allowed his posting to the empire to deprive him of initiative, to make him fatalistic, or to lead him to sleep on the job, had become *vertuerkt,* or "turkified." In quite elementary situations, those officers who had come to modernize the Turkish army found themselves facing problems that resulted from deep cultural differences. In such a rudimentary matter as uttering commands on a parade ground, for example, the monosyllabic half-scream favored by legions of Prussians since the eighteenth century did not have the same effect in the Ottoman Empire. The Turkish rank and file found it insulting to be addressed in this way. Ill will was generated, an ill will that intensified as less-tactful Germans found themselves unable to hide their contempt at the backwardness of their allies.

There was also the important question of the viability of Turkish troops in battle. Kress von Kressenstein, a German officer who demonstrated more than average understanding of Ottoman conditions, was placed in charge of a Turkish force sent to drive the English from Suez. En route, he made a courtesy call in Damascus on one member of the Young Turk triumvirate, Djemal, at that time enjoying a dual role as governor-general of Syria and minister of marine. Djemal told Kressenstein that his mission was bound to fail. When he was asked why, Djemal replied that Turks were good only in defense, not in attack.

A witty German officer observed, "In Turkey, that sense of order for which Germany is renowned, disappeared under the Southern sun."[4]

Even if the Germans had managed to bring the Ottoman army up to optimum fighting standards in a short time, the German military situation was further hampered by the multiplicity of command. One historian who has made a special study of this question commented,

> First there was the military mission under Liman von Sanders. Independent of this was the military attaché at the Embassy. Then there was General Bronsart von Schellendorf. Though he was theoretically a member of the military mission under Liman, he was Chief of the Turkish General Staff and therefore nearer to Enver and could rely on Enver's backing. Admiral Souchon, chief of the Mediterranean Division and Admiral Usedom, General Governor of

Coastal Defenses, were independent of the military mission. So was Field Marshal von der Goltz. If we add to this list also the Ambassador, who was also involved in military matters, the result is seven service operations (not including the influential naval attaché at the Embassy: Humann, so really eight) each of which had the right to send reports to the army headquarters and to Berlin. Wangenheim's attempt to get von der Goltz appointed as coordinator was a dead duck from the beginning."[5]

The one great achievement of the Turkish forces was in fact in defense, at the Dardanelles, as described earlier. As relations between Turks and Germans worsened, the Turkish voices reminding the Germans of the failed Allied initiative at the Straits became a steady chorus. We bailed you out at the Straits, said the Turks to the Germans. This was a reasonable retort, given the general disillusionment spreading within the German mission about the role of the Turkish army, a feeling they could not prevent from filtering through to the Turks. Even among the Australian and New Zealand troops of the enemy, the stubborn resistance mounted by the simple Turkish soldiers quickly earned them the sobriquet Johnny Turk—which may, of course, have been an unconscious attempt to demonstrate that the common soldier on both sides was a victim.

Liman, in charge of the 5th Army and the defense of the Dardanelles, received no praise from the general staff. It agreed he had prevented a major landing by the enemy and had given them no chance whatever to consolidate their position. But in late 1915 and early 1916, the Allied forces had been allowed to withdraw from the Gallipoli Peninsula without any loss of life; they did this at night under the eyes of the Turkish and German units and were not discovered. The leading

German officer at the end of the war, General Hans von Seeckt, not only considered Liman's defense of the Straits unimaginative (he felt that at best, Liman was a "plodder"), but Liman's failure to inflict damage on the enemy when they left was, in his view, unforgivable. Seeckt's opinions can be respected. During the 1920s it was he who built up a superb fighting force for Germany within the limitations prescribed by the Treaty of Versailles.

The senior German officials, whether in the army or in the diplomatic service, who came into contact and occasionally had to negotiate with Talaat and Enver needed special qualities. The two Young Turk leaders had their backs to the wall and treated diplomacy like a game of poker. They always called the bluff of the opponent. The Germans were at a disadvantage; knowing the importance of the alliance to their commander in chief, William II, they had to bend over backward to keep the precious liaison alive. The only person who did not waver in any dealings with the Turks (or anyone else, for that matter) was Liman. But he was motivated by other considerations. Was he being treated with the respect due to a senior German officer? This weighed much more heavily on him than the fate of the alliance. This was one of the reasons why Wangenheim could not abide him.

The Germans of this place and time in history have frequently been cast into the role of willing helpers of the Young Turks in their genocidal program against the Armenians. But this characterization is much more connected with the Germanophobia of the First World War than it is with the facts. It is true they were allied to the Turks, but even though there was a wide spectrum of behavior on the part of Germans in the heightened conditions of war, it is utterly misleading to consider them as helpers.

There is a curious central theme in the attitude toward Germans in the Ottoman Empire during the First World War. It is almost as though the reputation the Nazis earned in Europe during the 1940s is applied to a totally different historical period. This is nowhere better illustrated than in the story of Max Erwin von Scheubner-Richter.

This man found himself where history was being written at two places during two periods separated by only seven or eight years. We first met him as German consul at Erzurum, sending reports to his boss Wangenheim in 1915. The next time we meet him, his name appears as one of the early followers of Adolf Hitler during the abortive Munich Beer-Hall Putsch in 1923. Unfortunately, many people on seeing this juxtaposition develop the immediate equation German = Nazi = racist = exterminator. But the truth is infinitely more complex.

During his service at the German consulate at Erzurum, Scheubner-Richter saw firsthand the roundup of the Armenians. What he witnessed appalled him. On May 18, 1915, he cabled Wangenheim at the German embassy, "The misery of the deported Armenians is frightful. Women and children are camped around the town in their thousands without food. This pointless expulsion is causing huge bitterness. Will you authorize me to take steps with the army authorities?"[6]

Wangenheim's reply was cautious. Scheubner-Richter was told that he might go ahead, "But do not create the impression as if we want to exercise a right of protection over the Armenians or interfere with the activities of the authorities."[7]

This was hardly a green light. But on May 22, we find Scheubner-Richter cabling the embassy, "Spoke today by telephone with the Army about the deportation of the Armenians and shall visit HQ at Tortum Monday. Moslem emigrants are meanwhile occupying the villages of the Armenians who have been evicted."[8] Despite Wangenheim's very guarded reactions, Scheubner-Richter evidently tried to put pressure on the army authorities to step in and stop the depredations of the paramilitary formations driving the Armenians along the roads in their caravans.

On the second of June, he advised Wangenheim, "My conversations with the Commander in Chief did not lead to any positive result. It seems that the Armenian settlers of all the plains, including Erzurum, are to be sent to Deir-es-Zor. This large-scale evacuation is synonymous with massacre, for in the absence of any means of transport, hardly half of the refugees will reach their goal alive. . . . There can be no military reasons for this operation, because nobody envisages a revolt by Armenians here, and those driven away are old men, women and children. Those who convert to Islam are not evicted.[9] The deserted Armenian villages I visited had all been plundered."[10]

Wangenheim probably had no illusions about the scope and purpose of the operation. In any event, here was Scheubner-Richter announcing first that *resettlement* was a synonym for *murder,* and then that the plan had no grounding in military rationale. These were certainly not the verdicts of a man who sympathized with the plan to assassinate the Armenians. If we examine the types who associated with Hitler in his early days, we find they cover the gamut of Munich society of the time. Most of them wanted to prevent the Bolsheviks from reoccupying that city. It would be turning history on its head to suggest that they, even Scheubner-Richter, bear some responsibility for Hitler's subsequent racial programs.

Yet there is one area in which it is quite possible that Scheubner-Richter engaged the future führer's attention. It is clear that the events of the First World War were still dominant in the mind of the erstwhile German consul. It is certain that at one or another of the beer-hall sessions in which early members of the Nazi party indulged, Scheubner-Richter would have described the fate of the Armenians in wartime Turkey. No better source of information on their genocide could probably be found in Munich than the ex-consul, who was, incidentally, a reserve lieutenant in the German army. It is equally possible that the ideas of mass slaughter, no doubt already germinating in Hitler's tortuous brain, received a boost, a direction, once information about the Armenians had reached him.

For these reasons, Hitler's statement during his address to his generals before the invasion of Poland in 1939—"Who, after all, speaks today of the annihilation of the Armenians?"— has aroused widespread comment and speculation. An exhaustive study has even been written about the implications of this, in Hitler's view, rhetorical question.[11] In the light of Hitler's policies during World War II, surely we can agree that this dismissive attitude is fully consistent with his generally inhuman views about the disposal of unwanted minorities. Nonetheless, the quotation has aroused much comment, particularly among Armenians. Because of the continuous Turkish denials that the genocide ever took place, Armenians are forced to look for authentication wherever they find it. The fact is, however, that the genocide against the Armenians is established beyond doubt in a variety of original sources, not least of which are the captured coded cables sent from the center of the operation (the Ministry of the Interior under Talaat) to the outlying executives who were to put the plan into effect.

The reactions and behaviors among Germans to the genocide can be placed into two main categories. If they sat at the center of the seat of power in Berlin, they did little to rock the boat of the alliance with the Ottomans. If they were on the spot in some consular capacity, they tried to put a stop to the action. Examples of both types of behavior follow, yet the source material must be approached cautiously because of the prevalence of anti-German war hysteria at the time. For example, a German consul who intervened regularly to ease the lot of the Armenians was accused both in the British and American press of being a voluntary assistant in the genocide, a willing coworker of the Young Turks. In an age during which perfectly innocent Americans of German extraction were hounded in the United States, this is probably only to be expected.

Neither Wangenheim nor Margrave Johann von Pallavicini (the Austrian ambassador to the Sublime Porte) wanted to upset the applecart of the alliance. In a sense they were relieved when the Armenians mounted a defense at Van in April 1915, because it could be portrayed as evidence of an Armenian revolt and might provide some justification for the Turkish measures. Neither diplomat ever lost sight of the fact that their countries might be held accountable for the action against the Armenians. Wangenheim made a point of storing details in a special file each time he made an attempt to intercede; this was most likely done in the interests of postwar accountability.

On May 1, 1915, Pallavicini wired Vienna: "In view of the political significance which the question has . . . now assumed, I believe I should at the earliest opportunity alert the Turkish statesmen in a friendly manner to the repercussions which an inhuman proceeding against Christians in Turkey might have on the general situation; for our enemies will be given a new pretext to move with all their might against Turkey."[12] In view of the wholesale slaughter in which the Ottomans were engaged,

Pallavicini's suggestion that he "alert them in a friendly manner" is symptomatic of that general tendency of the Germans and Austrians not to offend their allies. Neither Wangenheim nor Pallavicini reacted to Ambassador Morgenthau's urgent plea that they put pressure on their respective governments to stop the genocide.

But in those areas of the empire in which the elimination of the Armenians was all too horrifyingly visible, Germans—be they in the consular service or working as educators, missionaries, or nurses—behaved quite differently.

On the eighteenth of May 1915, for example, Wangenheim received the following message from the German consulate at Adana: "The entire Armenian population of the *vilayet* Adana is in a state of extreme anxiety as a result of the actions of the Government. Hundreds of families have been deported, the prisons are overfull. This morning again many executions took place. Through its barbaric behavior the Government is publicly destroying all the assets of the country. The German Orient Bank, which has been severely damaged, has asked me to intercede to arrange the cessation of the deportation of the Armenians."[13]

From Mosul, the German consul cabled Wangenheim on June 10, 1915: "614 Armenian men, women and children sent here from Diarbekir have been murdered in rafts on the river; these rafts arrived here empty yesterday and for some days now bodies and human limbs have been floating by in the river. . . . I have told the local government about my deep aversion to this horrible crime. The *vali* expressed his sorrow and said that the *vali* of Diarbekir was responsible."[14]

The story of the much-abused German civil servant Consul Walter Roessler of Aleppo must also be told. As early as April 20, 1915, he informed Wangenheim that "the deportations are a misfortune for the country and are directed at an important section of the populace. They stem from a basic false premise, which is that the entire Armenian population may be viewed with suspicion, or entertains hostile feelings."[15] Some three weeks later, on May 10, Roessler wired, "The Government seems to proceed from the medieval standpoint that an entire race must pay for the actions of one individual member."[16]

Presumably with the agreement of Wangenheim, Roessler began to send copies of his cables to the German chancellor, Theobald von Bethmann-Hollweg. On June 6 he asked for German intercession: "Most of the deportees among the Armenians are women. In the caravans and in the villages they are easy prey for rapists. Would it be possible to evict only the men and let the women and children stay in Aleppo? Until now many children have not survived the caravans."[17] And on June 29 this vigorous proponent of humanitarian action cabled, "Zohrab and Vartkes Effendi, the two well-known Armenian Members of Parliament, are currently here on the caravan to Diarbekir. From what we know about this place, this means certain death. . . . I request permission to put in a word for them here so that they might stay in Aleppo."[18]

It is one of the ironies of the period that this consistent defender of the Armenians should have been the target of vilification in the British and American press. In London the Havas Agency issued a press release on September 30, 1915, in which it stated, "Several German Consuls have directed or encouraged the massacres against the Armenians. There is special mention of Mr. Roessler, Consul at Aleppo, who journeyed to Aintab to take over personal direction of the massacres."[19] Behind this story, apparently, was the correspondent of the *London Times* in Cairo. Was it, one wonders, the same journalist who accused U.S. Ambassador Morgenthau of being too busy protecting the Jewish community of Palestine to concern himself with the Armenians? Smearing one's enemy (or even one's ally) in wartime is a cheap way for any journalist to curry favor with readers. Such initiatives, which demonstrate the racism of the age, are utterly reprehensible.

Roessler's story is not yet completed. After some months of pleading for German intervention, he channeled a request directly to the German foreign office, sometimes referred to as the *Wilhelmstrasse.* Nothing symbolizes the difference between the consuls on the spot and the higher bureaucrats at the ministry as well as the following message, sent via Wangenheim to Roessler by Secretary of State Arthur Zimmermann: "The Embassy should seek to enlighten the consul, that despite the reprehensible machinations of the Armenians, efforts on their behalf have already been made."[20] In this way did Zimmermann put Roessler in his place. (Incidentally, this is the same Zimmermann who sent a notorious telegram telling the German ambassador in the United States to urge Mexico to invade U.S. territory if the United States entered the European war; the telegram was intercepted and, ironically, helped turn U.S. opinion against Germany and in favor of entry into the war.) We might assume that one of the consequences of Roessler's direct contact with Chancellor Bethmann-Hollweg was for the chancellor to put some pressure on Zimmermann. Zimmermann did not want this thorn in his side, and treated Roessler accordingly.

It was Zimmermann at the German foreign office who gave the most succinct summary of the "official" German position on the Armenian massacres. There was no question among many Germans that these massacres were taking place, and they had begun to receive notice in Germany. German missionaries, in their pastoral letters, and returning travelers who had seen ghastly things all gave reports that caused many people to sit up and take notice. A newspaper publisher who decided this was a delicate subject secured an appointment with Zimmermann to get some direction as to how to deal with the matter in his newspapers. He was told the following by the German secretary of state: "Without needing any prodding from church circles, the foreign office and the imperial representative agencies in Turkey have, of their own volition, already done all that was possible by diplomatic means to mitigate the sufferings of the Armenians. To bring about a break with Turkey on account of the Armenian question we did not and do not consider appropriate. For as regrettable as it is from the Christian standpoint that innocent people, too, must suffer under Turkish measures, the Armenians are after all less close to us than our own sons and brothers, whose sacrificial, bloody struggle in France and Russia is being indirectly aided by the military help of the Turks."[21]

It is difficult to like what one learns about Arthur Zimmermann from the historical records.

But it must not be assumed that all incumbents of the German embassy at Constantinople were such dedicated practitioners as he of a realpolitik in which German advantage took precedence over questions of genocide. Some have maintained that Wangenheim's death in the fall of 1915 resulted from a possible crisis of conscience on this issue. One of his successors, Count Wolff-Metternich, who was ambassador from November 15, 1915, to October 3, 1916, sent a report to the German chancellor (who felt himself in a vice on the Armenian question) in which he stated: "People like Talaat and Enver are well aware of the fact that the war effort is undermined when obstacles are placed in the way of railroad construction, but here nobody any longer has the authority to place restraints on the many-headed hydra of the Committee, with its chauvinism and fanaticism. The last of the Armenians must be cleaned out and the Government has to give in. The Committee's influence extends over all the *vilayets*. Every official from *vali* down to *kaimakam* has a Committee representative at his side, to support him or simply to watch him."[22]

Enver and Talaat quickly got wind of the critical eyes of Wangenheim's successor at the German embassy. They asked Berlin to replace him. This was done in late September 1916. The interim ambassador sent to replace the troublesome Wolff-Metternich, Prince Ernst zu Hohenlohe-Langenburg, actually delivered a message to the Porte on his own initiative. He said (without clearing this with his government) he had to "remonstrate again against these acts of horror and to decline all responsibility for the consequences which might spring from them."[23] Talaat, who read the note, said he would attempt to "curb the excesses of subordinate authorities." This was his way of passing responsibility on to a small group of officials at the fringes of the operation.

Despite some laudatory efforts on the part of German officials, the generally ineffective nature of German resistance to the genocide cannot be denied. Yet there is one personality who, almost single-handedly, restores the German image in this regard.

This person is Johannes Lepsius, who from 1896 until his death in 1926 did not fail to promote the Armenian cause, working in a consistent, upright, and dedicated manner. He was by profession a Protestant pastor. He had spent three months in Armenia in 1896, having been informed by colleagues of the Hamidian massacres. From this time on he made the fate of the Armenians his abiding activity. Prior to his departure for Turkey in 1896, Lepsius had become associated with the Deutsche Orient Mission, under whose aegis he founded two orphanages in the Armenian provinces from funds he and his associates had collected in their charitable work. On his return to Germany, Lepsius became a devoted voice for the Armenians of the Ottoman Empire. In this activity, he found that he ran counter to the prevailing tendencies in both governmental and church circles. These tended to minimize the importance of the treatment meted out to the Armenians, in view of William II's efforts to further German economic expansion in the Ottoman Empire. This did not deter Lepsius, who in 1897 published his *Armenien und Europa (Armenia and Europe)*, which was translated into English and French and was widely circulated in Germany.[24]

Biographical details in the introduction of his book justly laud what he accomplished: "Looked at with suspicion by the authorities, ignored by the press, he initiated a campaign of enlightenment with meetings, lectures and articles which were published anonymously in the conservative evangelical newspaper *Reichsbote*. He also requested a leave of absence from his parish, which was denied him. Shortly thereafter he decided to leave his pastorate, which meant giving up pension rights from the Evangelical Church. . . . At 38 years old he had found the real duty of his life, which took precedence over all other matters and for which he continued to enlist the support of others throughout his life."[25]

Lepsius's work took him frequently to Asia Minor and once evidence of the genocide filtered through to Germany in the spring and summer of 1915, he went to Turkey again. Here he managed to obtain an audience with Enver, at which he attempted to induce Enver to abandon his program of annihilation of the Armenians. According to the summary in his book,

"Immediately on his return on 30 September 1915 he sent a petition to the Chancellor, composed a memorandum for the German Foreign Office, addressed the Press Club in the German Parliament and published anonymous reports in Swiss newspapers about the persecutions of the Armenians." The chancellor's reactions were dilatory; the government preferred to remain silent in this matter, and the exigencies of censorship precluded any open publicity. Lepsius decided to write a report that would cover all the information he had gathered. Twenty thousand copies were distributed, personally addressed. The *Report on the Situation of the Armenians in Turkey* was confiscated, and those copies addressed to members of parliament were not delivered. The documents were published only after the war in 1919, under the title *Death March of the Armenian People*. After its publication Lepsius came under considerable attack; his own mission attempted to distance itself from his report, and for these reasons as well as problems of health, Lepsius took his family to Holland.

Only after the cessation of hostilities did he return to Germany. He then approached the new secretary of state, named Solf, to ask permission to see all the official documents (including those from embassies, consulates, and so forth) that had some bearing on the fate of the Armenians. This permission was granted. For a time Lepsius maintained a desk at the German foreign office, where he contributed to the mammoth research required for the publication of *Die Grosse Politik der Europaeischen Kabinette* (the official history of the prewar governmental action of all the European cabinets).

From this brief review of German attitudes and actions in relation to the Armenian genocide, it is apparent that generalization is difficult. But in a wider historical sense it can be argued that the Germans have no more reason to chastise themselves than do the British, the French, or the Americans. Were the Germans worse than the British, who simply, for reasons we shall examine, gave up on their promise to bring the guilty to trial? Do the French have a clearer conscience, when their abandonment of Cilicia freed nationalist forces in the new Turkey to slaughter the remaining Armenians there? And what of the Americans, who in the postwar atmosphere of isolationism failed to take the opportunity of taking over a mandate for Armenia, and thereby consigned the remaining Armenians to further depredations?

The central thing about genocides is that with each day of delay, while negotiators negotiate and politicians politick, thousands of innocent human beings are slaughtered. This is the final brutal fact of genocide.

Chapter 11

THE SLAUGHTER CONTINUES

If Lepsius's table is taken as a guide, only a couple of months separated the beginning and end of the genocidal action against the Armenians administered centrally by the Young Turk regime. Lepsius claims that the official operation began with roundups in Erzurum in mid-June 1915 and ended with a massacre in Urfa on August 19.

It may be considered splitting hairs to maintain that the genocide ended in August 1915. An Armenian dead at the hands of regular or irregular Turkish forces, no matter when, is still an Armenian casualty. But the initial policy, centrally administered by the Ministry of the Interior under Talaat and executed under the stewardship of Shakir within the *Teshkilati Mahsusa*, was considered fulfilled by the end of that year; what followed was, in Turkish eyes, a necessary by-product of military campaigns, despite the huge number of women, children, and the aged among its victims.

The accounting of the genocide is numbing. The Armenian leaders estimated the number of Armenians in the Ottoman Empire before the outbreak of the First World War at between 1.5 and 2 million souls. According to a reliable source, "Of these about 250,000 managed to escape to Russia either overland or by sea. Of the remaining 1,600,000 about 1,000,000 were killed, half of whom were women and children. Of the surviving 600,000 about 200,000 were forcibly Islamised; and the wretched remnant of 400,000 was found, starving and in rags, by the Allies . . . at the end of the War."[1]

By the beginning of 1917 huge numbers of Armenians had already died, either by mass butchery at the hands of the military and paramilitary units or as a result of starvation or disease. Many at the brink of death awaited their final moments in the Syrian Desert.

Nazim's warning in February 1915 to the Secret Committee of the *Ittihadists*—that one remaining Armenian represented a danger to the future of Turkey—proved prescient. There were survivors. They hung on in the most appalling conditions and had as their objective nothing other than the wish to stay alive. Their best chance of achieving this was to escape the wrath of Turkish arms by entering those areas of Caucasia and Transcaucasia still occupied by the forces of tsarist Russia. Armenians not on the verge of death therefore prized one attribute more than any other: mobility. Mobility meant the chance of safety, and safety meant life.

But once again, events were to take place in some other part of the world that would redound to the disadvantage of the tattered remnants of this ancient folk. In March of 1915 the Armenians had borne the brunt of the Allied decision not to seize the moment and push through to Constantinople. This decision, based on considerations other than the fate of the Armenians, nonetheless sealed their doom. This time the major event, with catastrophic consequences for the Armenians, was the Russian Revolution of 1917.

Armenians were aware it was Russian forces that would protect them from the Ottoman effort to annihilate them. But this Russian protection had a price. The administration of Russian Transcaucasia had recently pursued its characteristic steamroller attitude in its treatment of Armenians. The Russian government wanted to force the Armenians into the straitjacket of Russian Orthodoxy, and of late it had attempted to restrict the Armenians' freedom to assemble and to use their own language. It also insisted that Armenians produce title deeds, which none of them could find, attesting to their ownership of property to which they were attempting to return. Nonetheless, even though Turkish Armenian refugees—and there were around three hundred thousand of them—felt they were being abused by their tsarist overlords, it was better than slaughter.

The revolution in Russia in February 1917 was greeted with enthusiasm by most of the residents of Transcaucasia. Its exponents had loudly proclaimed their aversion to "bourgeois imperialism." This meant, to the various nationalities of the Caucasus (Georgians, Azerbaijanis, and Armenians), that perhaps some form of autonomy might replace tsarist hegemony. The new Russia, if its leaders were to be believed, would not indulge in imperialism. By the end of the winter of 1917, about 150,000 Armenians had returned to Erzurum, Trebizond, Van, and Bitlis, now under the control of Russian troops. In the words of an Armenian historian, "This apparent Armenian resurgence had been sanctioned and supported by the Petrograd

Provisional Government."[2] Furthermore, the revolution "eliminated the Tsarist restrictions and gave the Armenians the opportunity to gain valuable experience in the administration of Turkish Armenia."[3]

However, there was an element within the radical Bolshevik leadership whose views concealed a huge danger for the residual Armenians. Lenin not only wanted to remove his own war-weary country from the battlefields, but he was certain that the proletariat of all the warring nations, on whichever side, was waiting for a signal from the Bolsheviks to put down its arms and, by fomenting revolutions locally in each country, internationalize what was happening in Marxist Russia. Lenin had written that what had happened to the Armenians was the result of competing imperialisms. Their fate had hitherto been sealed because they were the victims of British, tsarist Russian, and French expansionism in that area. It would certainly not be the policy of the new Russia to perpetuate this. The Armenians together with the other minorities in the Caucasus should remain free to pursue their own self-government.

In late June of 1917, Lenin declared that he had no idea of the size of Russian forces on the Turkish front, but he assumed they totaled about 3 million soldiers. These units, Lenin asserted, were based in Armenia and continued to attempt to annex neighboring territories while advocating peace without annexation to other actors in the area. How much better it would be, Lenin declared, if the Russian army were to aim at creating an independent Armenian republic. This would then receive the financial backing from Russia currently "being taken from us by the Anglo-French financiers."[4] This dig at the hated imperialists, made before the total collapse of tsarist Russia, illustrates the extent to which Marxist orthodoxy colored the view of the Bolsheviks as to the future of the minorities of the Caucasus. Whatever its doctrinal virtues for them, it ignored the fact that if Russian forces withdrew from historic Armenia, they would be replaced by Ottoman armies bent on continuing the annihilation of all Armenians.

The abandonment of Armenia by Bolshevik Russia left the Armenians again at the mercy of the Turkish forces. The tension within the Russian army between officers and soldiers rapidly escalated, and Russian units soon were decimated by desertion in those areas they had acquired in the war. At the negotiating tables at Brest-Litovsk, where the conditions of peace were established between Russia's new rulers and the officials of the Central Powers, among the loudest voices were those of the Young Turks, who under Enver's continuous guidance, pursued Turkey's plan to enter Transcaucasia and put into effect its plan for unifying the areas between the Caucasus and central Asia under the banner of Turan. It was the Germans who had defeated Russia; it was the Turks who insisted on becoming the beneficiaries of this situation. The German secretary of state, Richard von Kühlmann, asked the Turks to moderate their requests, and he warned them that if they did not, they might get nothing.[5]

But all Young Turk sentiment pointed to an extension of empire across the Caucasus. It was here that Enver had intended to make his play during the failed campaign of winter 1914–15. Now Enver and his followers happily abandoned the notion of empire their predecessors had developed. With Transcaucasia in sight, who needed North Africa, Egypt, or Arabia, areas only associated with Turkish failure?

"Give this cursed desert to the English!" cried Enver's uncle, Halil Pasha, after the appallingly organized Turkish attempt to unseat the English at Suez. "Let us go to Turkestan, where I can found a new empire for my son!"[6] The *Ittihadists* were giving up their slender hold on the vestiges of the empire to the south and southwest; there, the Arabs had joined forces with the British. The Turkish future pointed to Transcaucasia.

The exit of Russia from the war gave an enormous boost to Turanism. There would now no longer be the troops of a historical enemy to act as a brake on Enver's wish to implement the Turanian idea. In the last year of the war, 1918, Ottoman efforts in the Caucasus and beyond were described in the newspapers of Constantinople as "The Liberation of our Brothers." In April 1918 the foreign minister of the National Government of the Crimean Turks (an association that owed its existence to the collapse of the tsarist empire) received a tumultuous ovation when, before a huge crowd in Constantinople, he announced, "We were one. We became one again and we shall always remain one." At the same meeting, another invitee of the *Ittihadists*, Mehmed Emin Resulzade, a leading Azerbaijani, proclaimed, "The youth of Azerbaijan will always stand at your side." These were stirring words for nationalist Turks, and a welcome change from the prewar days when the Young Turk administration was beset with problems arising from the wish of most of the empire's minorities to secure their freedom from the Ottoman Turks.

Those representatives of the Armenians trying to salvage what they could during the final months of the war were conscious of one fact above all: Armenia could not make it alone. It needed the protection of a foreign power to save it from the Turks. In the last year before the armistice, therefore, Armenian representatives tried to curry favor with all types of different groups. For a few months in 1918, a Transcaucasian Republic was established, comprised of Georgians, Azerbaijanis, and Armenians; it was thought that these three groups might advance the cause of their independence by acting in common. The endeavor failed from the start, mainly because there was no common denominator. The Azerbaijanis were by now committed to an understanding with the Turks, the Georgians managed to persuade the Germans to take up their cause, and the Armenians were once again left in isolation, an isolation beset with starvation, disease, and further tribulation wherever they met Turkish units. Their representatives were forced to make repeated attempts to secure German or Austrian or Russian assistance. For a while, there was an Armenian delegation of the Transcaucasian Republic in Berlin, where it attempted to put some pressure on the German foreign office to intercede on behalf of the Armenian people. As an example of its activities, in April 1918 the German foreign office received a wire from the Armenian delegation in Berlin that read: "As the highest authority of the Armenian people, the Armenian National Council now turns to you in the present insupportable situation. . . . Turkish forces have poured over our defenseless land, using the retreat of the Russian troops as their opportunity. They are murdering all Armenians, whether of Russian or Turkish origin. Responsibility for the fate of Armenians now rests in German hands. . . . It is due to German action that Russian forces have now left the area . . . and it is now Germany's duty to restrain the excesses of the Turkish troops. . . . We cannot believe that a great nation such as Germany could permit the peace terms at Brest to expose the Armenian nation—drawn into this conflict against its wishes—to countless sufferings."[7]

When this wire was sent in the spring of 1918, the *Wilhelmstrasse* was well-informed about Turkish excesses, but the German foreign office remained mealymouthed in its reactions. Nonetheless, an effort from very important quarters in Germany was mounted to intercede for the Armenians. No less a personality than the war hero (and subsequent president) Field Marshal von Hindenburg actually cabled Enver on July 19, 1918: "Various reports confirm that there is an urgent necessity to permit the return of Armenian refugees to Armenia so that they can bring in the harvest. Otherwise hundreds of thousands will die of starvation. Your Excellency will understand if, as a Christian, I intercede to prevent the starvation and death of 500,000 co-religionists. I urge Your Excellency, in the interests of humanity, to issue the order so that these unhappy people may be allowed to return to their homeland."[8]

On August 3, Enver replied: "To my great regret compelling military reasons prevent me from acceding to Your Excellency's request. . . . While it is not our intention to wage war against an entire population . . . Your Excellency is asking me to permit half a million partly armed people to exist in the rear of our fighting troops."[9] Of course, a war was being waged against an entire people, a fact of which Hindenburg was undoubtedly aware, yet here again the Young Turks simply went their own way, demonstrating, as they had done repeatedly, how little attention they paid to their German allies.

In partial defense of Enver's reaction, it must be admitted that a new factor had entered the situation. Among Armenians retreating from the Turkish advance into Russian-occupied Caucasia were some Armenian troops that, as they rapidly left areas in the path of this advance, did some killing of their own. In one scholar's words, "The frenzied troops and bands retreating from Erzurum killed any Moslems falling into their hands and burned the Turkish villages that lay in their path."[10]

News of this action by Armenian units swiftly reached the ears of German officers. Their chief spokesperson and leading officer in Turkey at the time, General Hans von Seeckt, commented, "For every story I hear about a Turkish atrocity, I hear about ten committed by Armenians."[11]

As recently as 1959, an official of the Turkish consulate general in the United States likened the disposition of the Armenians within the Ottoman Empire to that of Americans of German origin who were sympathetic to Germany's cause in the First World War. These Americans, he claimed, acted as a Fifth Column on behalf of Germany within the United States. Of course, there is one missing element that he studiously ignored—Americans of German origin were not slaughtered by the hundreds of thousands in the two decades before the war. It is, therefore, hardly a parallel case, but characteristic of Turkish attitudes since the First World War.

No restraints were imposed on Turkish forces. What this meant to the Armenian inhabitants of Baku in September 1918 was all too clear in a report sent by Lieutenant Colonel Paraquin, a German officer attached to Turkish Army Group East, to General von Seeckt:

> Entry through the suburbs of Baku presented a bizarre picture. The streets were almost empty of people. Almost without exception the shops and houses had been ransacked. At various points on the streets piles of objects had been gathered together. These appeared to have been deposited by Tatar plunderers and were occasionally guarded by individual Turkish soldiers. . . . Two murdered children lay on the street, and near to us a shot could be

heard in a side street. From a window we heard women screaming in desperation for help.

Nuri Pasha, commanding officer at Baku, made no attempt to protect Christian and European life and property. . . . Against all Turkish claims to represent the events at Baku as harmless and simply the natural consequence of storming the town, I have to say that the butchery had been anticipated weeks before and was put into effect with no reference whatever to tactical necessity.[12]

The units that committed these excesses were in fact mostly made up of Azerbaijani volunteers, who had been released on the town before it was formally occupied so that they might rape and plunder in keeping with the ancient principle "To the victor, the spoils." It has been assessed that, toward the end of the war, no fewer than 400,000 Turks had deserted from the Ottoman army, but obviously enough remained for Enver to enforce his will in Transcaucasia.

In the last months of the war between 50,000 and 100,000 Armenians were massacred by Turkish troops in the various Caucasus campaigns. To this figure must be added the results of genocidal actions taken by Turkish nationalist forces in Cilicia under Mustafa Kemal after the Mudros Armistice (October 30, 1918).

The Transcaucasian Republic disintegrated, as we have seen, as Georgia and Azerbaijan pursued their own interests. Armenia, now reduced to a small area around Yerevan, could do nothing other than declare itself an independent republic, which it did on May 28, 1918. By early August this republic consisted of some 750,000 Armenians already settled there plus somewhere between 300,000 and 400,000 refugees from west Armenia. This tiny area (in relation to historical Armenia) was the only area the Armenians could call their own, because of the existence of Turkish forces. The president of the Armenian National Council, Avetis Aharonian, reported on their status as follows:

> You cannot imagine the incredible proportions assumed by the flight of our nation and how appalling the misery caused. A single sea of Armenian refugees covers the roads between Yerevan to Dilidjan and Neubayazid. The army route between Tiflis and Vladikavkas is covered with fleeing Armenians. . . . The 80,000 Armenians of Achalkalai are compressed within the canyons of Bakuriani marooned and at the mercy of the official and unofficial authorities. The valleys of Karakilissa are full of refugees. Here are assembled all the Armenian residents of the districts of Kars and Alexandropol. Emboldened by the presence of Turkish troops, Tatars from Kaash and Bortshalu have perpetrated the most inhuman butchery against them. In the district of Karakilissa alone they murdered 2000 Armenians. At the station at Ashaghaserail, Armenian orphans who filled several wagons were butchered together with their teachers. The railroad between Karakalissa and Tiflis has become the slaughterhouse of our nation. . . . The crowd of refugees . . . disappears in misery . . . daily and hourly.[13]

"Armenia is hermetically sealed off everywhere by the Turks," so cabled General Friedrich Kress von Kressenstein to the German chancellor on August 4, 1918, "thereby making any exchange or contact with the outside impossible."[14]

A final indignity awaited the leaders of the crisis-ridden Armenian Republic. In the absence of any friends in high places or any support from the surrounding nations, they had to do something to formulate a living arrangement with the Turks, even if this meant expressing feelings of friendship for the very leaders of the genocide. According to one scholar, the Armenian leaders "felt the greatest revulsion to their acts of obeisance when performed before Enver and Talaat Pasha."[15] To complete this nauseating picture, "Talaat lamented the misfortune that had befallen the Armenians. He blamed the Kurds, the military and irresponsible local administration for the calamity."[16]

There must, however, have been some among the Armenians, despite the bloody reign of terror of the previous years, who derived some consolation or experienced some hope for the future in the knowledge that the days of the *Ittihadists* were limited. The war was clearly over, and would formally be declared so shortly.

Had not the leading politicians of the victorious Allies, of Britain, France, and the United States, declared unambiguously that they supported the rights of Armenia? Was it not clear that the innocent would be protected and the guilty brought to trial?

Chapter 12

In Pursuit of Justice

Serene and unhampered by enemy fire, ships of the Allied Aegean fleet, led by the British dreadnought *Superb*, made their way up the Dardanelles toward the Sea of Marmara and Constantinople on November 18, 1918.

It was three years and eight months to the day since their predecessors had experienced their inglorious failure in an identical exercise. In the war that had just ended, deaths on the Allied side amounted to some 5,152,000. For the Central Powers, the figure was approximately 3,386,000. These figures were mind-boggling to strategists raised in prewar conditions.

The figure given for Armenian casualties during the genocide varied between 600,000 and 1,500,000. Apologists for the Ottoman position tried to allude to these deaths as simply one more figure within the general constellation of the war, but one of the great differences between Armenian losses and those of other nations was the fact that most of the Armenian victims were women and children. In addition, when the Allied vessels reached Constantinople, the Armenian tragedy was far from over—in various parts of the empire, the number of survivors was diminishing daily as a result of starvation, disease, and continued slaughter.

Nonetheless, those Armenians capable of taking stock and thinking of the future, despite the trauma of the war years, felt they could derive some consolation from the unambiguous support of all the major participants in the Allied cause. As a starting point, they could review the exact wording of an Allied declaration made on May 24, 1915, an early testimony, surely, of Allied resolve in this matter—and equally a demonstration of the excellent links the Allied powers still had with information sources in the Ottoman Empire. There was no doubt that whatever the *Ittihadists* had undertaken by way of the slaughter of Armenians, news had reached England, France, and the United States within days, and this during a period of wartime censorship. The actual wording of the Allied message was as follows:

> For about the last month, the Kurds and the Turkish populations of Armenia have been engaged in massacring the Armenians with the connivance and often assistance of the Ottoman authorities. Such massacres took place about the middle of April at Erzurum, Tercan, Bitlis, Mous, Sassun, Zeytoun and in all Cilicia.
>
> Inhabitants of about 100 villages near Van were all assassinated. In the town itself the Armenian quarter is besieged by Kurds. At the same time the Ottoman Government at Constantinople rages against the innocent Armenian population.
>
> In view of these new crimes committed by Turkey, the Allied Governments announce publicly to the Sublime Porte that they will hold all the members of the Ottoman

Government, as well as such of their agents as are implicated, personally responsible for such massacres.[1]

Not yet able to prove that the conspiracy emanated from the center of the Young Turk regime, the Allied note alluded to the "assistance of the Ottoman authorities"; time was to prove that this assistance did not occur simply in some cases, but was a continuous feature of the *Ittihadist* scheme. Furthermore, the reference to the Kurds might blind the reader to the general recruitment of *cetes* for the purpose of forming paramilitary formations to escort and massacre members of the Armenian caravans. These were made up of not only Kurds, but Muslims from various areas of the Caucasus and from Transcaucasia, who made common purpose with the Young Turks. There were even Chechens involved.

If there was considerable optimism among surviving Armenians, it was not unfounded, for the resolve of the Allied powers to address the question of Armenia had not diminished since their declaration of 1915. Indeed, leading politicians in the Allied camp rarely failed to reconfirm their outrage at what had happened to the Armenians of the Ottoman Empire.

In England, for example, Prime Minister David Lloyd George "frequently promised that Armenia would never again be subjected to 'the blasting tyranny of the Turk,' and in a statement of his cabinet's war aims in January 1918, repeated that 'Arabia, Armenia, Mesopotamia, Syria and Palestine are in our judgment entitled to a recognition of their separate national condition.' In August of that year he told an Armenian deputation 'Britain will not forget its responsibilities toward your martyred race.' Numerous similar pronouncements were made before Lloyd George summarized the official British attitude: 'From the moment war was declared, there was not a

British statesman of any party who did not have it in mind that if we succeeded in defeating this inhuman Empire, one essential condition of the peace we should impose was the redemption of the Armenian valleys forever from the bloody misrule with which they had been stained by the infamies of the Turk."[2] Lloyd George, apart from being a highly articulate politician with a large following in the country, was also a lawyer. One wonders what he meant by his list of countries (Arabia, Armenia, Mesopotamia, Syria, and Palestine) being "in our judgment entitled to a recognition of their separate national condition." Could this be taken to mean that England would support their total autonomy? Or was the wording left intentionally vague so as to leave open other possibilities? In any event, no Armenian could read the speech without feeling that Britain would stand behind any Armenian attempt to arrange gradual or immediate self-government.

From France, the auguries were equally bathed in sunshine. In November 1916, Premier Aristide Briand wrote: "When the hour for legitimate reparation shall have struck, France will not forget the terrible trials of the Armenians, and in accord with her allies she will take the necessary measures to ensure for Armenia a life of peace and progress." And in July 1918 Prime Minister Georges Clemenceau wrote to Bughos Nubar, president of the Armenian National Delegation: "I am happy to confirm to you that the Government of the Republic, like that of Great Britain, has not ceased to place the Armenian nation among the peoples whose fate the Allies intend to settle according to the supreme laws of Humanity and Justice."[3]

How many Armenian activists, still alive despite the slaughter, must have compared these generous and unambiguous sentiments to the rejections they suffered in prewar times when they went, cap in hand, from one power to another looking for support? Surely even the most hardened and experienced negotiator might be excused for seeing the Armenian future with some optimism.

No less encouraging were the sentiments expressed in the United States. At the forefront of American policy were President Wilson's Fourteen Points, which if put into practice, must surely guarantee an independent homeland for surviving Armenians, even if this were secured under a mandate from one of the powers. America had certainly been lavish in its attempts to collect funds for distribution to the Armenians, for whose fate there was general sympathy throughout the nation. This was in part due to the reports circulated by members of American religious missions and also because of the active pen of the erstwhile ambassador Henry Morgenthau, which had inflamed anti-Turkish sentiment in every corner of the nation. Under the heading "Ambassador Morgenthau's Story," the magazine *World's Work,* in its issue of November 1918, carried an article of his that is typical of what Turks have subsequently labeled Turcophobia. It is worth quoting at some length because of its effect on the Western reader and its tendency to polarize Turkish and Western viewpoints:

> Such graces of civilization as the Turk has acquired in five centuries have practically all been taken from the subject peoples whom he so greatly despises. His religion comes from the Arabs; his language has acquired a certain literary value by borrowing certain Arabic and Persian elements; and his writing is Arabic. Constantinople's finest architectural monument, the mosque of St. Sophia, was originally a Christian church, and all so-called Turkish architecture is derived from the Byzantine. The mechanism of business and industry has always rested in the hands of the subject peoples, Greeks, Jews, Armenians and Arabs. The Turks

have learned little of European art or science, they have established very few educational institutions and illiteracy is the prevailing rule. In the north-eastern part of Asia-Minor, bordering on Russia, there were six provinces in which the Armenians formed the largest element in the population. From the time of Herodotus this portion of Asia has borne the name of Armenia. The Armenians of the present day are the direct descendants of the people who inhabited the country three thousand years ago. Everywhere they are known for their industry, their intelligence and their decent and orderly lives. They are so superior to the Turks intellectually and morally that much of the business and industry has passed into their hands. With the Greeks, the Armenians constitute the economic strength of the Empire.

As we saw much earlier, this view of the Ottomans, of the Turks, was common in the West. (In England there was only one exception, and that was the voice of the Right Honorable Aubrey Herbert, who for years led a pro-Turkish lobby in the British House of Commons.) The general consensus was that the Turks had behaved abominably and the Armenians deserved a home of their own and as much Western support as could be enlisted in their cause.

This was sensed and digested by the successors to the Young Turks. Clearly, representatives of the discredited regime of Talaat and Enver could not meet the British at the negotiating table to discuss the terms of the armistice. Other Ottomans less likely to offend the conquerors had to be found. Talaat Pasha's government had resigned on October 7, 1918, with Talaat himself resigning as grand vizier and Enver as minister of war on October 13. The sultan approached Izzet Pasha (the same individual who had met Liman on day one of Liman's tour of duty in December 1913) to act as successor. Izzet thereupon assumed the offices of prime minister and minister of war and appointed a commission to negotiate an armistice. In a meeting of the Central Committee of the Committee of Union and Progress he convoked on November 1, 1918, Talaat recommended the dissolution of the party. A few hours later, in the company of other leading members of the Young Turk movement, he left by ship for Odessa, whence they made their way to Germany, where asylum had been granted to them. On board this vessel were, in addition to Talaat, Enver and Nazim and Shakir. That their influence would survive their departure from Constantinople will become abundantly clear.

Meanwhile, as leading members of the victorious Allied powers, the British were under strong pressure to make good on their pledge to try those guilty of atrocities against the Armenians. Together with other officials from other governments, they set up high commissions in Constantinople and staffed them with political officers—largely civil servants who had experience in some other branch of the British bureaucracy, in the foreign service, colonial service, or War Office, for example—whose function was to collect testimony, statements, and affidavits relating to those Ottomans against whom legal suit might be brought.

At the same time, the administration of Izzet Pasha, mindful of the need for Turkey to appear in a good light at the negotiating tables of the peace conference, determined that the successors to the Young Turks must be seen to be making an attempt to punish the guilty. Shortly after signing the Mudros Armistice of October 30, 1918, Izzet Pasha's cabinet passed a resolution to prosecute the leading members of the *Ittihad ve Teraki* party. It must not be overlooked that within Turkey there had been dissidents, and that according to one commentator "courageous individuals had not only spoken out against the massacre of the Armenians, but had balked at implementing the secret directives of the Committee of Union and Progress."[4]

To proceed, a hunt for incriminating documents, for testimonies that might be used, was begun. If they existed, they would be found in abundance at the various wartime ministries. But there was a major difficulty in collecting them. These ministries were still staffed with supporters of the Committee of Union and Progress, many of whom considered that those being sought for trial were among the nation's most dedicated patriots. As one scholar has observed, "Supporters and sympathizers of the C.U.P. still dominated the Civil Service, the War Office and particularly the police, whose pervasive presence was a primary factor in inhibiting the investigation and prosecution of the culpable."[5]

There was also a knotty problem of jurisdiction. Under which system of law should the trials take place? International law? British law? There was in place none of the machinery that would become available during the Nuremberg trials some thirty years later. Meanwhile within Turkey itself an attempt was made to invoke a procedure granted by the constitution in which a deputy could file allegations of misconduct against a minister. An Arab deputy announced his willingness to enter a motion to try Enver and Talaat in this way in the high court. But such was the continued strength of erstwhile *Ittihadists* in the chamber that they managed to thwart this action. The sultan, still anxious to prove to the world that Turkey was able to try its own criminals, dissolved the chamber. On March 8, 1919, he authorized the setting up of an Extraordinary Courts Martial with competence to try those accused of being involved in the genocide against the Armenians.

Thus it was that from early in 1919 there were two main organizations intent on proceeding against the guilty. At the British high commission instituted in Constantinople, depositions were made, information gathered, and minutes exchanged with London (especially with the law officers of the Crown) as to how best to proceed from a legal standpoint. The Turkish Extraordinary Courts Martial also assiduously gathered the documentation necessary for the preparation of trials. We shall deal separately with their respective histories, starting with the British. (This is not to diminish similar efforts mounted, for example, by the French, but the one put into effect by the British was far more wide-ranging.)

For the British installed at the high commission, the question of the trials of those involved in outrages against the Armenians was but one of a series of preoccupations. In fact, they had prepared a list that formed the basis of a series of inquiries conducted by the British foreign office together with the law officers of the Crown. The list covered the following categories:

a. Failure of Turks to comply with the terms of the armistice
b. Impeding the execution of armistice terms
c. Insolence to British commanders and officers
d. Ill-treatment of prisoners
e. Outrages to Armenians or other subject races in Turkey and Transcaucasia
f. Participation in looting, destruction of property, etc.
g. Any other breaches of the laws and customs of war

Categories (e) and (f) were of relevance to the Armenian situation. The British continued to arrest and detain suspects, but British relations with France began to deteriorate badly, and the possibility of some concerted action between the Allies receded daily. France became increasingly suspicious of British policies in the Middle East, a suspicion that was generously reciprocated in Britain. Early in 1920 a high-ranking official of the British high commission, Sir Harry Lamb, sent a report to the foreign office in which he maintained the following: "It appears to me that unless there is wholehearted co-operation among the Allies, the trials will fall to the ground and the direct and indirect massacrers of about one million Christians will get off unscathed. Rather than this should happen, it were better that the Allies had never made their declarations in the matter and had never followed up their declarations by the arrests and deportations that have been made."[6]

Despite this gloomy view, the work of the British high commission continued apace, as is evidenced by this memorandum from the second political officer, Andrew Ryan, written on November 14, 1920: "In practice we have gone on the principle that a sufficient presumption of guilt to justify detention and ultimate prosecution existed against all members of the responsible Government of Turkey at the time when the massacres and deportations took place and all persons so high in the councils of the C.U.P. as to be able to be credited with a share in directing its policy. . . . Pending further developments I think we should keep any ex-ministers who certainly formed part of Turkish cabinets when the deportation and massacre policy was adopted and carried out. . . . In one sense the question is a juridical one and not one of policy at all. So far as it is a question of policy I suppose it is one of Allied Policy. I take it that all prisoners now held on any ground connected with deportations and massacres must be regarded as held in trust for the Allied Powers."[7]

This suggests that there was still some resolve among those whose duty was to arrange the prosecutions. Unfortunately, this resolve was not shared at home in the House of Commons. It was item (d), the ill-treatment of prisoners, that began to exert a greater influence on the discussions about Turkey, rather than what should be done about bringing guilty Turks to trial.

One thing is clear: Given the overwhelming wish to demobilize the forces, no Allied government that attempted to extend military service would have survived a general election at home. But if the Allied powers did not increase their military presence in the Ottoman Empire, there were huge areas that would remain outside their control. This meant that British and French forces in Anatolia were limited to certain relatively small areas. This in turn meant that the initiatives taken by Kemal Atatürk, now heading a Turkish army in Ankara, were outside of Allied control. Gradually, Kemal had gathered around him all the nationalist forces in the empire. He went his own way and issued his own decrees, to the delight of most Ottoman patriots and the despair of the de jure Ottoman government in Constantinople.

Among the great assets Kemal Atatürk enjoyed was the possession of some twenty-nine British prisoners of war, including a certain Colonel Rawlinson. He had been repeatedly urged by the British authorities to release these prisoners, and he had repeatedly refused to do so unless the British, in return, released those Ottomans they held in custody awaiting trial. These prisoners of war became Kemal Atatürk's bargaining chip. Suspicious of the efficacy of Turkish security measures at the prison in which the detainees were held, the British had arranged their removal to the British colony of Malta. These were the men Kemal wanted returned to him; it was an issue on which he would not budge.

Questions were continuously asked in the House of Commons about the fate of these British prisoners of war. It became a very delicate political issue. The overwhelming body of opinion in England was in favor of a trade; although most of the British prisoners in question were sepoys (natives of India fighting for the British), Colonel Rawlinson was a constant concern. The fact that the British were holding some 150 Turks at Malta, most of whom were involved in the execution of the genocide, in no way affected the crude arithmetic of this exercise. Pressure was put on the English government to secure the release of the prisoners. One foreign office official commented injudiciously on the outcome in a memo: "I had to explain why we released the Turkish deportees from Malta, skating over thin ice as quickly as I could. There would have been a row, I think. . . . The staunch belief among Members of Parliament is that one British prisoner is worth a shipload of Turks, and so the exchange was executed."[8] This situation indicated at an early stage how political exigencies would come to determine whether or not the Armenians would see their persecutors tried in court.

Political exigencies also helped to promote the career of Kemal Atatürk from his base in Ankara. One circumstance in particular aided his ascendancy in Turkey after the First World War, and its centrality to our theme makes it necessary to allude to it before we consider the trials held by the Turks themselves.

Any wavering political sentiment among Turks hardened immediately when in May 1919 a Greek force occupied Smyrna (now Izmir). Eleuthérios Venizélos, the Greek representative at the peace conference, had managed to persuade Britain and France that Greek forces were immediately needed in this area to combat the marauding Turks, who were decimating the Christian population in and around that city. In fact, no evidence was offered in support of this claim, but the Allies acceded to the Greek request. The behavior of the Greek troops, once landed, was appalling. Huge numbers of innocent Turks were slaughtered. In Constantinople a massive crowd of more than 200,000 people assembled in a demonstration against Greece. In this explosive situation, the strong and intractable attitude of Kemal Atatürk seemed the only course open to most patriotic Turks, who felt that the League of Nations had failed to live up to its promises in not crushing this Greek action. The star of Kemal Atatürk began to rise from this moment; he offered a much more palatable image of behavior than the weak government at Constantinople, which the ordinary Turk began to view as a government of sycophants. Once the British had released their prisoners—in what must even today be regarded as one of the more spineless examples of British policy—they no longer had recourse to legal action. The information that the officials at the British high commission had gathered by way of incriminating material, affidavits, statements, and eyewitness reports remained under lock and key at the Public Records Office outside London until the statute of limitations on the materials recently expired, permitting their release for inspection.

The defection of Britain in the area of pursuing guilty Ottomans left history with only the verdicts arrived at by the Extraordinary Courts Martial. Hardly anybody has had a good word to say about these trials, which we must now examine. There were two types of prejudices at work in the public assessment of the proceedings of the courts martial. The more cynical evaluation came from foreigners, who insisted that the only function of the trials was to give the Turkish delegation to the peace conference in France a better bargaining position. Within Turkey itself, a noisy faction protested that there could be no question of collective guilt, and that the Turkish nation itself appeared to be on trial. Furthermore, those apprehended were—so it was claimed—among the most patriotic members of the nation.

The position, therefore, of the president and members of the court was very problematical. They were all high-ranking regular army officers. One can imagine the pressure they were under once the Greeks had invaded Smyrna, an act that gave resurgent Turkish nationalism a huge boost and turned ever more eyes to Ankara, where an increasingly obdurate Kemal Atatürk continued to fulminate against the unfairness of the Allies. The trials began in Constantinople on April 27, 1919, and ended, after some pauses, on June 28, 1919. Fortunately, the court's proceedings were published each day in the official gazette *Takvimi Vekayi,* a journal that has since been suppressed by the Turkish authorities (since it would only lend substance to Armenian claims). But the Armenian leaders in Jerusalem kept copies of the gazette, to which scholars have since had access.

The "big seven" among the accused (Talaat, Enver, Djemal, Nazim, Shakir, Bedri, and Jemal Azmi) were tried in absentia, since most of them had escaped to Germany, where despite initiatives from both the Turkish and British governments, the authorities refused to release them.

The indictments prepared and verdicts rendered by the court contain sufficient incriminatory evidence to prove conspiracy to commit genocide. At the trial of several of the big seven, the indictment read: "The key finding of this investigation shows that the criminal acts that took place at various times and in various places, during the deportations of the Armenians, were not isolated, local incidents but were premeditated and realized by the oral instructions and secret orders of the 'Special Center.'"[9] This is vital in any case that has as its subject genocide; it must be shown that there was centrality of purpose and execution. Here, a Turkish court is admitting precisely this. Furthermore, according to the indictment, "The nature of *Teshkilati Mahsusa,* which was initially created by the leaders of *Ittihad ve Teraki,* was, as the evidence clearly shows, especially secretive, and its real aim was to commit criminal acts. This secret network was led by Central Committee members Dr. Nazim, Behaeddin Shakir, Atif, Riza and former Director of Public Security Aziz Bey. The headquarters of Behaeddin Shakir were in Erzurum, from where he directed the forces of the Eastern *Vilayets.*"[10] These are of course, the *vilayets* of heaviest Armenian settlement.

What of the rest of the incriminating documents? In his indictment, the prosecutor continued, "The Inquiry revealed that important documents relating to the Central Committee of the Party and to the *Teshkilati Mahsusa* were removed. Similarly reliable witnesses certified that before the dismissal of Talaat Bey, directives and other important correspondence sent from the Interior Ministry to Aziz Bey, former Director of the Ministry of Public Security, were not returned."[11] This will not surprise any student of the period; when you have in mind to destroy an entire community, you leave behind as little documentation as possible. Therefore, the recent statement (mentioned earlier) by Bernard Lewis—that the genocide against the Armenians in the Ottoman Empire is not substantiated in the documents available for study—must be seen in a very guarded light. Most such documents were destroyed. In any event, the existence of many authenticated telegrams sent to outlying areas proves the case.

One of the most important areas investigated by the court was the question of the connection between the party organization of the Committee of Union and Progress and the local executives of the genocide. In this area, the function of the responsible secretaries was vital. These were the party officials responsible for party affairs in each *vilayet*. (In Nazi Germany they were called *gauleiters*.) Despite every effort, it became well-nigh impossible for the prosecutor actually to pin down any of those on trial as to the connection between the party and the genocide. Those indicted were adept at sidestepping such questions. But one absolutely invaluable piece of evidence (which we have already quoted) was in the form of a cable sent by Shakir to the responsible secretary of Harput, in which he asked: "Are your area's deported Armenians being liquidated? Are the dangerous people you mentioned being destroyed? Or are they being merely deported and exiled? Clarify this point, my brother."[12] One cannot avoid asking, If the *Ittihadist* party was not involved, why was Shakir asking this question of its chief spokesperson in Harput? If there was any doubt about the fact that deportation meant annihilation, it was surely dispelled by this telegram.

The existence of these telegrams is central to our understanding of the massacres. The court's inspectors exercised the precaution of having an appropriate official write "This is a true copy of the original" on each piece of incriminating material as it was collected. This showed considerable prescience on their part; doubters cannot now argue that authenticated documents do not exist.

The documentary evidence was far more persuasive than that provided by oral interrogation. When Cevat Bey, military governor of Constantinople during the war years, was cross-examined by the president of the court, the following exchange took place:

> PRESIDENT: What were the duties of Dr. Nazim and his colleagues, that you mentioned earlier?

CEVAT BEY: They were engaged in the matter of recruiting volunteers. That is why they were there.

PRESIDENT: What were their links with you?

CEVAT BEY: There were no links whatever, Effendi [a Turkish title of respect].

PRESIDENT: If there were no links, why were they with you?

CEVAT BEY: They were not with us.

PRESIDENT: I mean with you in your offices.

CEVAT BEY: They were at the offices of *Teshkilati Mahsusa*.

PRESIDENT: Did you not ever go there?

CEVAT BEY: I went there very rarely.

PRESIDENT: Did they not meet with you while you were coming and going?

CEVAT BEY: Yes, they used to meet with me.

PRESIDENT: Regarding what matters?

CEVAT BEY: Regarding sending certain individuals or volunteer detachments to the Caucasus.

PRESIDENT: How could these individuals be directing these affairs when they were not even in the military?

CEVAT BEY: It is probable they were recruiting volunteers who had no connection with military personnel.[13]

In this and in many other examples throughout the trials, the accused showed themselves to be masters at dissembling and befogging issues. Nonetheless, during its brief life, the Extraordinary Courts Martial tried and condemned to death the big seven and passed sentence on many others. But these sentences were too light to satisfy the need for retribution felt by many in both Armenian and Allied circles. The acting high commissioner for England at Constantinople, Rear Admiral Richard Webb, stated: "It is interesting to see . . . the manner in which the sentences have been apportioned among the absent and the present so as to effect a minimum of real bloodshed."[14] The fact that the leading exponents of the genocide lay beyond the court's ability to exact its punishment was shortly afterward remedied by Armenian radicals. But before we address the vengeance of these radicals on the chief perpetrators of the genocide, we must consider the fate of the Armenians in Cilicia.

The Armenians of Cilicia were involved in a life-and-death struggle that prevented them from applying themselves to the pursuit of justice. The sentences passed by the Extraordinary Courts Martial were delivered in January of 1920, but by this time the Armenians in Cilicia had their attention riveted elsewhere. It was clear from the actions of Kemal Atatürk and the nationalists that they considered the retention of the whole of Anatolia as the irreducible minimum of the new Turkish state. It had become Kemal's avowed intention to expunge the area of all foreigners. This included the occupation forces of all foreign powers, be they from France, England, or Greece. For the Armenian population of Cilicia, this meant that the need for Allied protection was paramount. Some 150,000 Armenians had managed to survive the death marches that terminated at Deir-es-Zor in the Syrian Desert. They hung grimly on to life. The Allies recommended their return to Cilicia under Allied supervision. The Muslim population of Cilicia was well aware that at the peace conference, Armenian delegations, flushed with optimism, had submitted plans that would reserve for Armenia the entire area of the eastern *vilayets* together with Cilicia, or Little Armenia. Therefore Muslim sentiment was resentful and inflamed. Given the pro-Armenian atmosphere at the peace conference, it looked to them as if what they considered to be their country might be taken away from them.

Moving huge numbers of surviving Armenians was possible only with the strongest Allied supervision. At first General Edmund Allenby, the victorious British general, sent a British force to escort the survivors and to act as a policing force in Cilicia. This worked well. But in due course the British left and were replaced by a smaller French force, which counted among its units some very determined Armenians who had joined the French during the course of the war. It was this French force that Kemal attacked with his nationalist army. In Marash, the French mounted a vigorous defense, and Kemal was on the point of withdrawing to regroup when a surprising event took place. During the cover of night, the French withdrew, even though they were on the point of victory. This action left the recently resettled Armenians at the mercy of the nationalist forces. The result was their annihilation.

What happened? Why did the French withdraw? Most analysts refer to secret meetings between French foreign official Georges Picot and Kemal in Ankara. Here, in exchange for certain economic and strategic advantages, Picot announced that France would withdraw its forces from Cilicia. The leader of the Turkish nationalists agreed to this arrangement, and this accounts for the departure of the only protection the Armenians had: the French forces.

The British, who, jointly with France had arranged the accord of 1916 in which British and French areas of influence and control had been delineated, were aghast. It had been part of their agreement that no changes would be entertained without first securing the approval of the other partner. It was also significant that Picot had negotiated with Kemal instead of with the de jure government in Constantinople. It was a slap in the face to that government and especially to Britain, France's wartime ally. Because of these developments, in 1920 Sir Harry Lamb announced, as we have noted, that without agreement between the wartime allies, the proceedings against war criminals would lose their driving force.

Once again the Armenians had become the legatees of political developments not of their making. Over eleven thousand Armenians in Marash alone were annihilated by nationalist troops. With the French out of the way, Kemal continued to cleanse Cilicia of foreign troops, with corresponding effect on the many Armenians there. For those Armenians who managed to escape death, the results of the trials in Constantinople were of marginal interest only, taking second place to the question of how to stay alive. This was, however, not true of certain activists within the Armenian *Dashnak* party.

These activists had seen how the major criminals had sought and obtained asylum in Germany. They had seen how that country refused to send these men back to Turkey to stand trial, despite repeated overtures from both the Allies and the weak de jure government at Constantinople. The chief architects of the genocide were at liberty to plot and regroup abroad. Something had to be done. It was a matter of self-respect.

According to Yves Ternon, one of the leading French historians of the Armenians, "The technique of *Dashnak* terrorism was copied from the battle structure of the Russian Social Revolutionary Party, which was itself inherited from the populists. The group operated on the fringes of the Party, under the supervision of a leader. Its membership did not go beyond ten persons and it took action only after extensive training. After the target had been found and positively identified, he would be placed under surveillance to chart his movements. Then, at the first opportunity, the execution would take place. . . . Added to this identity of technique was an identity of behavior. The Armenian avenger in the 1920s identified with his plan, sublimated it. He hated murder, but sacrificed his life. His action was felt as a vital necessity. . . . Once the decision had been taken by the Party, the victim was already killed, as if the terrorist incarnated the bullet that was to hit him."[15]

It is clear that whoever the party designated as the assassin simply accepted that death might be the price to be paid.

To arrange and execute the first of the attacks, that on erstwhile Grand Vizier Talaat, the party designated Soghomon Tehlirian. He succeeded in his assignment in Berlin on March 15, 1921. His trial, widely reported and attended, took place in Berlin on June 2–3, 1921.

In another age and in another set of historical circumstances, Tehlirian's background would have aroused consternation. Unfortunately, what befell this young man was almost ordinary during the course of the Armenian genocide. A participant, together with other members of his family, in one of the forced marches typical of that era, he was hit on the head with an ax and left for dead by one of the Turkish gendarmes. When he regained consciousness he gradually became aware that on top of and around him were the corpses of fellow Armenians, also abandoned on the roadside, among whom were members of his own family. Once Tehlirian became mobile, he sought to escape the area, generally traveling at night to avoid detection.[16]

There were physical consequences to the blow he received, as well as psychological ones resulting from his ordeal. He underwent attacks of a form of epilepsy, but these did not prevent him from being the sort of dedicated material the radical

Dashnaks could make use of. He was twenty-four years old when he assassinated Talaat.

At his trial some two and a half months later, he was cross-examined by the presiding justice, and among other statements, he informed the court as follows:

> PRESIDING JUSTICE: How did your parents, brothers and sisters die?
>
> DEFENDANT: As soon as the group had gone a little distance from the city, it was stopped. The gendarmes began to rob us. They wanted to take our money and anything else of value that we had.
>
> PRESIDING JUSTICE: Therefore, even the soldiers were robbing the deportees?
>
> DEFENDANT: Yes.
>
> PRESIDING JUSTICE: What reason was given for those acts?
>
> DEFENDANT: Nothing was said about that. It is inexplicable to the whole world, but in the interiors of Asia Minor it is possible.
>
> PRESIDING JUSTICE: First you said it was the guards, gendarmes and cavalry soldiers who attacked you, but then you said the mob attacked you. What do you mean by this?
>
> DEFENDANT: The Turkish population of Erzinga.
>
> PRESIDING JUSTICE: Then the Turkish population was there and took part in the robbery?
>
> DEFENDANT: All I know is that when the gendarmes started the massacres, the Turkish population fell upon us.[17]

The significance of these statements is that they were being made in an open court attended by journalists, which therefore provided an unparalleled opportunity for an Armenian to tell his story—and Tehlirian appeared to be telling the truth. He stressed how later he had been assisted by some Kurds. "Those Kurds were very kind people," he asserted, "They advised me to go to Persia. They gave me old Kurdish clothes as mine were torn and bloodstained. I burned mine." Given the way in which the Kurdish cavalry units had decimated the Armenians in the 1896–97 assaults under Abdül-hamīd, it might have been expected that Tehlirian would start from the premise that there were no good Kurds. Such was not the case, and it lent authenticity to his testimony.

The trial also provided an excellent opportunity for Johannes Lepsius, who was called as an expert witness, to speak with authority on the whole question of the treatment of the Armenians by the Ottomans. In answer to a query from the presiding justice, Lepsius stated, "The plan for the deportation of the Armenians was decided upon by the Young Turk Committee. On this Committee were Talaat Pasha as minister of the interior and Enver Pasha as the minister of war. Talaat gave the orders and, with the help of the Young Turk committee, implemented the plan. Already by April 1915 the deportation or general exile had been decided upon. It affected the entire Armenian population in Turkey with a few exceptions." During the same summary, Lepsius continued, "Whether in 1895–96 or in 1915, it was the same class of Armenian merchants living in Constantinople, Smyrna and Aleppo that escaped the massacres, partly because they were able to pay ransom. On the other hand, the entire rural Armenian population of Eastern Anatolia, which comprised 80 percent of the total Armenian population, as well as the tradesmen, who were mostly Armenians, were sent to the desert and annihilated."

It took the jury only one hour to pronounce a not guilty verdict, which produced considerable commotion and applause among the spectators. One German newspaper, the socialist *Vorwaerts*, announced that although it was not in favor of political assassination, Tehlirian might be compared with the legendary Swiss hero, William Tell.

Further assassinations by activists from the *Dashnak* party were soon carried out. On April 17, 1922, Behaeddin Shakir and Jemal Azmi were liquidated in Berlin, and in May of that year Enver Pasha was killed while serving with the Soviets. (Enver's death occurred in central Asia and was not part of the general program called Operation Nemesis.) In July 1922, Ahmed Djemal was gunned down in Tiflis.

The success of the assassinations notwithstanding, one commentator, a lawyer, has observed: "There is no real substitute for trial in an open court, in which testimony can be assessed, amplified, refuted, in which all the paraphernalia of the judicial process can be brought to bear on the issues which determine culpability. And herein lies the secondary tragedy of the first genocidal action of the twentieth century. . . . Today's Armenians have to live not only with the fact that their forebears were mercilessly slain, but they also have to swallow the pill of decades of denial that the events ever happened, denial voiced by the successors to the regime of the Young Turks who engineered the mass murders."[18]

The *Dashnak* party continues to seek retribution for the massacres of 1915, even today. As recently as the 1970s and 1980s, *Dashnak* leaders took part in the assassination of forty-one Turkish leaders. The party opposes any relations with Turkey until it receives a formal apology for the killings, and it claims that eastern Turkey is legitimately part of a greater Armenia.[19]

Chapter 13

GENOCIDE AND THE TWENTIETH CENTURY

The dominant cause of violent death in the twentieth century has been genocide. According to one source, more than 119 million people have died as a result of genocidal acts since 1900. This is nearly 84 million more people than were killed in both world wars plus all the revolutionary and civil wars in this century.[1] Yet there is little we have been able to do to control it.

Unlike the feverish search underway to find methods of controlling the spread of AIDS, the search for ways to halt the use of genocide as a political weapon cannot be sought in scientific laboratories. Genocide does not lend itself to the sort of analysis used so effectively in the natural sciences. Rather, it is in the fields of history and the social sciences that most of the work relating to genocide must be done. These disciplines are hampered by a central handicap: History does not repeat itself, and therefore what we learn about one genocide does not necessarily assist us in understanding another. However brilliantly a scholar describes how and why a genocide took place in one arena, any attempt to use these findings in another is beset with problems.

There are, of course, similarities between genocides. Robert F. Melson, in an attempt to make a comparative study between the genocides of the Armenians and the Jews, has pointed to a common factor: A racial community that has traditionally been despised evokes even more hatred when it shows itself more able than the majority to adjust to huge social changes, such as industrialization or urbanization.[2] In Nazi Germany and in the Ottoman Empire, the rapid economic success and progress of previously despised communities engendered further hatred. This was true of attitudes toward both Armenians and Jews but it is doubtful if it throws any light on, say, the recent genocide in Rwanda.

The search for common elements, central to a scientific study, founders because genocides exist for only a limited time in a limited area. The settings are vastly different. The onslaught against the Armenians took place in a society that was unbelievably backward in relation to that of Germany of the 1930s and 1940s.

This basic inability to isolate a list of causes common to all genocides has dogged the study of the subject for two generations. When details of the most widely known and most recorded genocide, that of the Nazis against the Jews, became public, it was to the social sciences and social psychology that most scholars turned. Through these disciplines, so it was thought during and immediately after World War II, we would come to understand the slaughter. Intensive study would show us how to set up a causology for genocide. We would be able to see it coming. We would be able to do something about it. And we would have the legal machinery in place to impose our will on those perpetrating it. As early as December 11, 1946, the United Nations Convention on the Prevention and Punishment of the Crime of Genocide announced that genocide was a "crime under international law, contrary to the spirit and aims of the United Nations and condemned by the civilised world."

The scholarship on the subject of genocide grew out of the general shock and horror evoked by the sight of piles of bodies at Auschwitz. One leading analyst of genocide, Israel Charny, produced a book with the title *How Can We Commit the Unthinkable? Genocide: The Human Cancer.* In it , the author says: "If there has been any attempt at a sensible explanation of genocide over the years, it has been along the lines of understanding how historical, political and economic forces build to legitimate destructiveness in the name of this or that national, religious, racial or whatever group purpose. Nothing of what I have been saying is intended in any way to dismiss or minimize the critical significance of these large-scale sociohistorical processes. The problem is that these large-scale events in themselves do not really explain the ultimate human phenomenon of man's ability to destroy his fellow man."[3] Charny would doubtless argue that the foregoing history of the Armenian genocide provides no answers to the questions he poses regarding human brutality.

Does our inability to produce a satisfactory comparative method for the study of genocide mean we should abandon the attempt to understand it? Not at all, argues another scholar.

In a very interesting essay, Nora Levin suggests that each genocide can be studied in its own terms. We can abandon comparative yardsticks as to causes and still learn much about the subject. She contends, "Each tragic history, I believe, deserves its
own study."[4]

Levin also introduces the issue of the perception of the
survivors of a genocide and the effect this may have on what is
written about it. She argues that each genocide "will seem
unique to those who identify with it and should not be in taste-
less competition for first place in uniqueness or intensity of suffering. We are not scoring points in debate. We are trying to
comprehend the shadowy histories of victimized peoples." In
addition to pointing out the problems of methodology surrounding the study of genocide, Levin reminds us of the attitude of survivors who believe most urgently in the uniqueness
of their racial or national experience. Both these points of view
detract from setting up a genuinely comparative study based
on methods that might, however loosely, be labeled scientific.
"I want each specific mass annihilation to be understood in its
own specific context," argues Levin, "not melded into a layer of
horrors. No amount of psychosocial structure building or compulsion to classify can distort the singular facts of history, theology and experience."[5]

While it is true that science needs generalizations to do its
work effectively, it was certainly not a compulsion to classify
that drove Melson to write his profound and scholarly *Revolution and Genocide*, in which he attempts to demonstrate the
common properties of the genocides against the Armenians
·and the Jews. He characterizes these as "total domestic genocides" and says similar genocides are "likely to occur only under circumstances of revolutions that lead to war and [are] not

likely to happen in other contexts. Thus revolutions that lead to war are among the necessary but not sufficient conditions for total domestic genocide."[6]

Melson's results are necessarily tentative and conditional. Where does this leave the layperson who wants to understand the causes of genocide? Though social scientists are not to be blamed for the limitations of their discipline, they leave the layperson floundering and possibly looking to other avenues of inquiry, for example to religion or philosophy, for some guidance.

The genocides perpetrated by the Young Turks and the Nazis do, however, clearly have certain features in common. As a matter of straightforward historical observation, it can be shown that there are striking similarities in organization and intent. These include the following:

Universality. No exceptions are made by the perpetrators of genocide. Although some of the wealthier Armenians in the cities were able to buy their way out of assassination, in large measure they shared the fate of their less wealthy compatriots. The order to kill covered every element of the society to be eliminated. Likewise, in Germany, those German Jews who had over the generations become more devoted patriots than the Germans themselves were not exempt; they were slaughtered with the rest. The parades of the Association of Jewish ex-Servicemen in the dying months of the Weimar Republic were pathetic because those marching thought that possession of the Iron Cross, earned in the trenches of the First World War, would save them from the vilification endured by the more recently arrived Jews from Poland. Such was not the case. Nor did their efforts at self-preservation produce the desired effect. At first they tried to prove their patriotism. Next they attempted to distance themselves from the eastern Jews who had entered Germany in the 1920s and who drew attention to their foreignness by speaking Yiddish and wearing foreign dress. None of this helped them in the face of the radical surgery advocated by Hitler.

Equally universal in scope and intention was the attitude of the predators toward young babes and even the unborn. The child emerging from its mother's womb was hated before it had even drawn breath. It was a public enemy and had to be eliminated. Therefore, off Trebizond on the Black Sea, Armenian infants were loaded into sacks and taken out to sea, where they were thrown in and drowned. In Germany, infants were eliminated by the Nazis to avert future dangers. The same reasoning, incidentally, was employed by some brutish types in the United States during the attacks on Mormons in the nineteenth century. In October 1838, writes historian Juanita Brooks, "A band of ruffians fell upon a little settlement at Haun's Mill. Some of the Mormons fled to the woods and took shelter in the brush, but a group hid in an old blacksmith shop, among them a number of children. Of this group, eighteen were killed and a number seriously wounded. When one small boy begged for his life, a mobocrat [member of one of the gangs that persecuted Mormons] answered, 'Nits make lice,' and blew out his brains."[7] As both Hitler and Nazim warned, children grow up to be enemies.

Contempt for Economics.   Genocide is also recognizable for its contempt for economic considerations. In view of their central importance to the economy of the Ottoman Empire, eliminating Armenians was inimical to the entire war effort. The number of jobs requiring skill or training that were held by Armenians was out of all proportion to their ratio of the population. Within a few months of the roundups, the signs of economic decay were everywhere. A Danish nurse at one of the mission schools wrote that it was impossible to get a roof repaired and that maintenance work of a general kind had simply ceased. This was a minor inconvenience, however, compared with the needs of the engineers involved in the construction of the Berlin-to-Baghdad railway. The continuous requests set by Talaat's Ministry of the Interior to the administration of the railway to release immediately their Armenian workers were ignored by the German directors. To accede would have meant the abandonment of one of the most important aspects of the war effort. But the purists among the Young Turks did their best to pursue this aim regardless of its economic cost. Franz J. Guenther, the German chair of the railway board, conducted a struggle with the ministry in which he maintained that to release the 850 Armenians at work on railroad construction would bring the work to an immediate halt.

Similarly, the rounding up of the Jews placed further strains on a German economy already stretched by wartime conditions, not to mention the adverse effects of the extensive diversion of railway stock to transport the victims to the assassination centers.

Organization.   To deserve the name, genocides must be centrally organized. This was the case in the Ottoman Empire, for research has now conclusively demonstrated that the operational nerve center of the genocide was the *Teshkilati Mahsusa,* which engaged the *cetes* and paramilitary units who were to escort and murder the members of the Armenian caravans. The continuous steering of the program was provided by Talaat at the Ministry of the Interior.

In Nazi Germany, representatives of the important ministries of the Third Reich were summoned to what has become known as the Wannsee Conference of January 1942. The purpose of this conference was to assemble the leading lights of the various ministries involved in putting into effect the extermination of the Jews. Adolf Eichmann, who basically acted as runner for the SS in putting the plan into practice, found himself in very elevated company. He took notes while he listened respectfully to the deliberations of, among others, Wilhelm Stuckart, undersecretary in the Ministry of the Interior; Undersecretary Josef Buehler, Hans Frank's assistant in the General Government of occupied Poland; and various representatives of Joachim von Ribbentrop's foreign office.

Here we see the gigantic differences of scale separating the backward, ill-organized, breathless Ottoman Empire and the systematic and logical German civil service. From our perspective, however, it is what they have in common that is significant. The annihilation of human beings, whether in a gas chamber in Poland or in the forsaken territory of the Mesopotamian Desert, is the common element.

Ideology.   Genocides normally have ideologies. The relative flimsiness of the Turanism provided by the Young Turks in comparison with the Aryan-race ideas of Nazi Germany is striking. But for whom would the Young Turks have provided an ideology? The vast mass of the Turks of Anatolia were illiterate. Certainly, whether or not Turkish peasants were moved by the notion of Turan, their grounding in militant Islamism could be relied on by the Young Turk leadership. The Muslim peasants would know, for example, that infidels must be taught their place. How different was the situation in Germany, where for at least a hundred years before the Nazis, the ideas of race, nation, and exclusiveness had been rapidly gaining ground. The Nazis did not superimpose racism on Germany; they simply extended and radicalized what was already there.

In any event, despite the fact that perpetrators of genocides need an ideology to legitimize their world views, it is a moot point whether or not this ideology is actually the motivating factor. "The Jews are our misfortune!" (Die Juden sind unser Unglück) announced that most nationalistic of nineteenth-century German historians, Heinrich von Treitschke, over a hundred years ago. But did this belief lead to the gas chambers? And did Turanism, so vital to Enver, induce Turkish or Kurdish peasants to kill Armenians?

While there can be no proof either way, some of the issues can be addressed. It is clear that in its early years and while gathering strength, any violent political faction must produce arguments that are persuasive to the men and women whose backing it seeks. We might call this an ideology. But to what extent does this produce the brutality common in genocide? Is a person wielding an ax animated by an ideology when the ax falls?

Do people need a *because* when they set out on indiscriminate murder? Do they need to know why they are doing it?

This question is addressed in a remarkable study by Christopher Browning called *Ordinary Men*. In his book, Browning traces the history of a battalion of reserve police officers from Hamburg detailed to assassinate Jews in a Polish village. He asks the question: How did a battalion of middle-aged German reserve police officers face the task of shooting some 1,500 Jews in the Polish village of Josefow in the summer of 1942? He makes it clear to us at the outset that these men were not specially trained for this task or considered particularly suited to it.

Browning sets the scene at Josefow. The men of the battalion were assembled before their commanding officer, Major Trapp. Down the road were the Jews, awaiting destruction. Trapp now had to issue his orders to his men. They had to be told to fire at random and slaughter the Jews. But at this point, Trapp experienced some difficulties. According to Browning, who interviewed witnesses of the event, Trapp, "pale and nervous, with choking voice and tears in his eyes, . . . visibly tried to control himself as he spoke. . . . There were Jews in the village of Josefow who were involved with the partisans, he explained, according to two others. The Jews had instigated the economic boycott that had damaged Germany. The battalion had been ordered to round up these Jews. The male Jews of working age were to be separated and taken to a work camp. The remaining Jews—the women, children and elderly—were to be shot on the spot by the battalion. Having explained what awaited his men, Trapp then made an extraordinary offer: if any of the older men among them did not feel up to the task that lay before him, he could step out."[8]

Trapp felt he had to appeal to ideology, to explain to his men why they were committing an atrocity. Yet from other sources we know that the main impetus to following such orders is peer pressure. This emerges clearly from interviews conducted by American and British psychologists with former German SS troops after World War II. The troops followed orders because they were anxious not to be seen as letting their buddies down. This has little to do with any ideological directive. Even during the height of the war in Germany, visiting lecturers would complain that the SS troops much preferred joining

German army units in beer-drinking sessions to sitting quietly while further quasiscientific monologues were conducted on the nature of Germanic runes or the latest findings on the history of the Aryan race.[9] All of this surely means that we must be very cautious in our evaluation of the importance of ideology to genocide.

The Macho Aftereffect. Those who perpetrate genocide generally view their male victims as passive or weak, certainly as somewhat less than manly. The Armenian male, forbidden to bear arms and more likely to become a businessman than a warrior, typifies this evaluation, as does his Jewish equivalent, who seemed to lack qualities of aggression.

After the genocides, surviving males have disproved these evaluations. The Armenian survivors systematically eradicate Turkish leaders, and the Jews (now for a large part, Israelis) display heroism and expertise on the field of battle. They are light-years away from the picture of helpless victims painted by their enemies.

This surely is one of the ironies of history. If Heinrich Himmler, who killed himself by swallowing a cyanide pill in 1945 after a lifetime of preaching the physical and moral superiority of the Aryan race, had by some strange means been able to revisit earth a generation or two later, what would he have made of his enemies, the Jews? For were not the survivors perfect examples of precisely the strong, vigorous, and determined types he had insisted on enrolling into his SS?

The indiscriminate slaughter of the innocent organized by the perpetrators of genocides produces behavioral changes in those who survive. If we look back to the quiet, inward-looking Armenian community in the Ottoman Empire of a century and a half ago, when it earned the description from the sultan of "my most loyal *millet,*" and compare it with the community of today, we can appreciate the radicalism of the change.

In this change, the intervening incidence of horror and barbarism called genocide has played a fundamental role.

Notes

Chapter 1. A General Arrives

1. Otto Liman von Sanders, *Five Years in Turkey* (Annapolis: United States Naval Institute, 1928), 2–3.

2. Ibid., 1, 2.

3. Ulrich Trumpener, *Germany and the Ottoman Empire, 1914–18* (Princeton, N.J.: Princeton University Press, 1968).

4. Ibid.

5. Liman von Sanders, 9.

Chapter 2. Turks and Armenians

1. J. A. R. Marriott, *The Eastern Question* (Oxford: Clarendon Press, 1919), 3.

2. Vahjakn Dadrian, "Genocide as a Problem of National and International Law," *Yale Journal of International Law* 14, no. 2 (summer 1989).

3. Ibid.

4. Sir Mark Sykes, *Through Five Turkish Provinces* (London, 1900).

5. In the German periodical *Der Spiegel*, no. 13 (1992).

6. D. Hogarth, *A Wandering Scholar in the Levant* (London, 1896), 89 et seq.

7. Justin McCarthy, *Muslims and Minorities: The Population of Ottoman Anatolia at the End of the Empire* (New York: New York University Press, 1983), 47–88.

8. Lord Kinross, *The Ottoman Centuries* (New York: Morrow Quill, 1977), 557.

9. Christopher J. Walker, *Armenia: The Survival of a Nation* (London, 1980), 137.

10. Ibid.

11. Ibid.

12. *British Foreign Office Documents,* ref. 424/184, no. 458/1, 126–128.

13. Ibid.

14. Ibid., ref. 424/184, no. 195/1.

15. B. M. Simsir, ed., in the introduction to *British Documents on Ottoman Armenians* (Ankara, 1990).

16. In the issue of the Young Turk journal *Mechveret,* of which Riza was editor.

17. Murat Bey, "La Force et la Faiblesse de la Turquie" (Geneva, 1897), as quoted in E. Ramsaur, *The Young Turks: Prelude to the Revolution of 1908* (Princeton, N.J.: Princeton University Press, 1957), 41.

18. Ibid., 10.

19. Walker, 170 et seq.

Chapter 3. Young Turks at the Helm

1. Lord Kinross, 583 et seq.

2. Johannes Lepsius, *Bericht ueber die Lage des armenischen Volkes in der Tuerkei* (Potsdam: Tempel Verlag, 1916), 18.

3. Lord Kinross, 583 et seq.

4. Much of this source material became available only recently. All governments close such files generally for 25, but in some cases 50 or more, years. All the powers that maintained em-

bassies at Constantinople in the last years of the Ottoman Empire have now opened their files for inspection and are a rich fund of source material for the student of the period. Especially useful are the documents now available in London, Berlin, and Vienna.

5. *Austrian State Archives,* political archive ref. HHStA PA XII, 462.

6. Ibid.

7. Ibid.

8. Ibid.

Chapter 4.   Which Way Will Turkey Go?

1. McCarthy, 47–88.

2. Lepsius, *Bericht ueber die Lage,* 162.

3. Richard G. Hovannisian, *Armenia on the Road to Independence* (Berkeley and Los Angeles: University of California Press, 1967), 42.

4. Liman von Sanders, 22.

5. Ibid.

6. Gaerayer Koutcharian, ed., *Siedlungsraum der Armenier* (Berlin: Free University of Berlin, 1989), 116.

7. Liman von Sanders, 39.

Chapter 5.   London, January 1915

1. Alan Moorehead, *Gallipoli* (New York: Harper and Brothers, 1956), 35.

2. This is not to be confused with first sea lord, a title usually given to Britain's leading sailor, at this time Lord Fisher.

3. Moorehead, 36.

4. *British Foreign Office Documents,* ref. 424/184, no. 558/1, 303.

5. Moorehead, 41.

6. This incident was first reported by Captain G. R. G. Allen, RN, Eady's son-in-law. It was the subject of an article in the *Royal United Service Institution* of May 1963.

7. As reported by Admiral W. M. James in his biography of Hall.

8. Moorehead, 77.

9. As quoted in Moorehead, 69.

Chapter 6. Constantinople, March 1915

1. This and additional information on Ambassador Morgenthau was gleaned from an address to the American Historical Association by Barbara Tuchman in December 1976.

2. Ibid.

3. Henry Morgenthau, *Ambassador Morgenthau's Story* (New York: Garden City, 1918), 187 et seq.

4. Lewis Einstein, *Inside Constantinople* (London: John Murray, 1917), xiii.

5. Liman von Sanders, 49–50.

6. Joseph Pomiankowski, *Der Zusammenbruch des Ottomanischen Reiches* (Zurich: Amalfeaverlag, 1928), 115 et seq. It should be mentioned that Pomiankowski attributes the sinking of the Allied vessels on March 18, 1915, to Turkish firepower, and not to mines. He also claims that the shore batteries had sufficient ammunition at the end of that day to withstand two more assaults.

7. Harry Stuermer, *Two Years in Constantinople* (New York: George H. Doran, 1917), 77.

Chapter 7. Preamble to a Genocide

1. Quoted (and translated) from "Procès des Unionistes: Documents microfilms de la bibliothèque du Congrès de Washington," in the appendix to *The Trial of Talaat Pasha,* stenographic

court records. Also to be found in Tessa Hofmann, *Der Voelkermord an den Armeniern vor Gericht: Der Prozess Talaat Pascha, Berlin 1921* (Vienna: Goettingen, 1980).

2. Vahjakn N. Dadrian, *The Role of Turkish Physicians in the World War I Genocide of Ottoman Armenians* (New York: Pergammon Press, 1986), 171.

3. G. S. Graber, *History of the SS* (London: Diamond Books, 1994), 76.

4. Gerayer Koucharian, *Siedlungsraum der Armenier* (Berlin: Free University of Berlin, 1989), 114.

Chapter 8. The Young Turks and Their Ideology

1. These comments of Paikert are taken from Gottfried Jaeschke, "Der Turanismus der Jungtuerken" in *Welt von Islam* (1937).

2. Lord Kinross, 614 et seq.

Chapter 9. Genocide

1. C. J. Walker, *Armenia: The Survival of a Nation* (London: Croom Helm, 1980), 202–203.

2. *British Foreign Office Documents*, ref. 371/6501.

3. Ibid.

4. Ibid.

5. Ibid.

6. Ibid.

7. This is a reference to Henry Morgenthau.

8. *British Foreign Office Documents*, ref. 371/6501.

9. Ibid.

10. Statement made in Turkish, translated into French (and subsequently into English) at the British high commission in Constantinople, *British Foreign Office Documents*, ref. 371/6501.

11. U.S. State Department record group 59,867.4016/72, as reported in *United States Official Documents on the Armenian Genocide,* vol. 1, ed. A. Sarafian, (Watertown, 1993).

12. Ibid.

13. Trumbull Higgins, *Churchill and the Dardanelles* (New York: Macmillan, 1963), 254.

14. Koucharian, 115.

15. Hofmann, 134.

16. Quoted in D. M. Lang, *The Armenians: A People in Exile* (London: Unwin, 1981), 31.

17. Harold Armstrong, *Turkey in Travail* (London: John Lane, 1925), 26.

18. Johannes Lepsius, *Deutschland und Armenien; Sammlung diplomatischer Aktenstuecken* (Bremen: Donat & Temmen, 1986), xxv.

Chapter 10. Germans and Turks, Germans and Armenians

1. Field Marshal von Hoetzendorf, *Aus Meiner Dienstzeit, 1906–18,* vol. 3 (1922), 612.

2. Ibid.

3. Quoted in J. L. Wallach, *Anatomie Einer Militaerhilfe* (Duesseldorf, 1976), 150.

4. Hans Guhr, *Als Tuerkischer Divisionskommander in Kleinasien* (Berlin, 1937), 30.

5. Wallach, 206.

6. Lepsius, *Deutschland und Armenien,* 73.

7. Trumpener, 207.

8. Lepsius, *Deutschland und Armenien,* 75.

9. Clearly, Talaat had not yet issued his circular banning the conversion of Armenians to Islam.

10. Lepsius, *Deutschland und Armenien,* 80.

11. This is the theme of a lengthy analysis in K. B. Bardakjian, *Hitler and the Armenian Genocide* (Cambridge, Mass.: Zoryan Institute, 1985).

12. Trumpener, 208.

13. Lepsius, *Deutschland und Armenien*, 73.

14. Ibid., 82.

15. Ibid., 49–50.

16. Ibid., 66.

17. Ibid., 81

18. Ibid., 93.

19. Ibid., 9.

20. Walker, 233.

21. Trumpener, 221–22.

22. Lepsius, *Deutschland und Armenien*, 277.

23. Ibid.

24. These biographical details are abstracted from Lepsius, *Deutschland und Armenien*.

25. Tessa Hofmann, introduction to *Deutschland und Armenien*, by Johannes Lepsius.

Chapter 11. The Slaughter Continues

1. Walker, 230.

2. Hovannisian, *Armenia on the Road to Independence*, 50–80.

3. Ibid.

4. Ibid.

5. Ibid.

6. Jaeschke, 1–50.

7. Lepsius, *Deutschland und Armenien*, 379.

8. Ibid., 416.

9. Ibid., 419.

10. Hovannisian, *Armenia on the Road to Independence*, 135.

11. Quoted in Friedrich von Rabenau, *Seeckt, aus seinem Leben 1918–1936* (Leipzig, 1941), 26.

12. Lepsius, *Deutschland und Armenien*, 441–42.

13. Ibid., 417.

14. Ibid., 420.

15. Hovannisian, *Armenia on the Road to Independence*, 231.

16. Ibid.

Chapter 12.   In Pursuit of Justice

1. Hapag Lloyd, *News Review*, May 24, 1915.

2. Richard G. Hovannisian, *The Armenian Holocaust: A Bibliography* (Cambridge, Mass.: Armenian Heritage Press, 1978), xiii.

3. Ibid.

4. V. Yeghiayan, *The Armenian Genocide and the Trials of the Young Turks* (La Verne, Calif.: American Armenian International College, 1990), xxiv.

5. Ibid.

6. From *British Foreign Office Dossiers on Turkish War Criminals,* (La Verne, Calif.: American Armenian International College, 1991).

7. Ibid.

8. *British Foreign Office Documents,* ref. 371/7882/E4425, 182.

9. *Takvimi Vekayi,* April 27, 1919.

10. Ibid.

11. Ibid.

12. Hofmann, 134.

13. *Takvimi Vekayi,* May 12, 1919.

14. Quoted in Dadrian, "Genocide as a Problem of National and International Law."

15. As quoted in Jacques Derogy, *Resistance and Revenge* (New Brunswick, N.J.: Transaction Publishers, 1990), xxvi.

16. It should be mentioned that some doubt about the authenticity of Tehlirian's story has been expressed by some historians. But this, so they claim, does not affect the genuineness of his mission. This position is taken, for example, by Edward Alexander in *A Crime of Vengeance*, (New York: Free Press, 1991).

17. Abstracted from the minutes of the trial in *The Case of Soghomon Tehlirian* (Los Angeles: ARF Varantian Gomideh, 1985).

18. Yeghiayan.

19. "Tough Armenian Leaders Make Allies in West Squirm," *New York Times*, November 11, 1995, A1.

Chapter 13.   Genocide and the Twentieth Century

1. Samuel Totten, "Teaching about Genocide," *Social Science Record* 24 (fall 1987).

2. Robert F. Melson, *Revolution and Genocide* (Chicago: University of Chicago Press, 1992).

3. Israel Charny, *How Can We Commit the Unthinkable? Genocide: The Human Cancer* (Boulder, Colo.: Westview Press, 1982), 23.

4. Nora Levin's essay appears in *Holocaust Literature*, ed. Saul Friedman (Westport, Conn., 1993).

5. Ibid.

6. Melson, 278 et seq.

7. Juanita Brooks, *The Mountain Meadows Massacre* (Norman: University of Oklahoma Press, 1987), 5.

8. Christopher Browning, *Ordinary Men* (New York, 1992).

9. G. S. Graber, *History of the SS* (London: Diamond Books, 1994).

Glossary

bey A courtesy title placed after a name.

Central Powers The wartime alliance of Germany and Austria-Hungary.

cete A brigand, recruited mainly by *Teshkilati Mahsusa* to escort and subsequently annihilate the Armenian columns.

Committee of Union and Progress (CUP) *See Ittihad ve Teraki.*

Dashnakstutium The most important of the Armenian political organizations, founded in 1890. Members were called *Dashnaks.*

dragoman An official at one of the foreign embassies at Constantinople, with a special knowledge of local language and customs.

effendi A Turkish title of respect.

grand vizier The leading political figure in the Ottoman Empire.

Hamideye Special paramilitary units founded by Abdülhamīd (and named after him), composed of Kurds dispatched to the Armenian *vilayets*. These units were largely responsible for the slaughter of Armenians in 1896–98.

Hunchak   A political party of the Armenians that, though slightly older than the *Dashnakstutium,* was eclipsed by it in importance.

Ittihadists   Members of the *Ittihad ve Teraki.* Also called *Young Turks.*

Ittihad ve Teraki   Turkish name for the Committee of Union and Progress (CUP), the political party of the Young Turks.

kaimakam   A commissioner of a subdistrict in the Ottoman Empire.

kaza   A subdistrict.

konak   A government building.

millet   A national or religious group within the Ottoman Empire.

mutassarif   A governor of a sub-*vilayet.*

pasha   A title placed after a name, formerly borne by civil and military officials of high rank.

Sharia   The canon law of Islam.

softa   Muslim theology students, generally studying for the priesthood.

Sublime Porte   The entrance to the Ottoman palace in Constantinople, which gave access to the grand vizier, who represented the government and the sultan. It came to signify the Ottoman government.

Takvimi Vekayi   An official gazette published by the government in Turkey.

Teshkilati Mahsusa   Turkish name for the Special Organization founded by Enver Pasha in August 1914 to execute the genocide against the Armenians.

Triple Entente   The wartime alliance between England, France, and Russia.

Turanism   The ideology of the Young Turks.

vali   The governor of a province.

vilayet   A province, the largest subdivision within the Ottoman Empire.

Young Turks   Members of the *Ittihad ve Teraki*. Also called *Ittihadists*.

RECOMMENDED FURTHER READING

Alexander, Edward. *A Crime of Vengeance: An Armenian Struggle for Justice.* New York: Free Press, 1991.

Arlen, Michael J. *Passage to Ararat.* New York: Farrar, Straus & Giroux, 1975.

Dadrian, Vahjakn N. "Genocide as a Problem of National and International Law: The World War I Armenian Case and Its Contemporary Legal Ramifications," *Yale Journal of International Law* 14 (1989): 221–334.

———. *History of the Armenian Genocide: Ethnic Conflict from the Balkans to the Caucasus.* Providence, RI: Berghahn Books, 1995.

Hovannisian, Richard G. *Armenia on the Road to Independence.* Berkeley and Los Angeles: University of California Press, 1967.

———, ed. *The Armenian Genocide: History, Politics, and Ethics.* New York: St. Martin's Press, 1992.

Kerr, Stanley E. *The Lions of Marash: Personal Experiences with Armenian Near-East Relief, 1919–1922.* Albany: State University of New York Press, 1973.

Kinross, Lord. *The Ottoman Centuries: The Rise and Fall of the Turkish Empire.* New York: Morrow Quill, 1977.

Lang, David M. *The Armenians: A People in Exile.* London: Unwin Paperbacks, 1988.

Lewis, Bernard. *The Emergence of Modern Turkey*. London: Oxford University Press, 1968.

Marsden, Philip. *The Crossing Place: A Journey among the Armenians*. New York: Kodansha International, 1995.

Miller, Donald E. and Lorna Touryan Miller. *Survivors: An Oral History of the Armenian Genocide*. Berkeley and Los Angeles: University of California Press, 1993.

Walker, Christopher J. *Armenia: The Survival of a Nation*. London: Croom Helm, 1980.

INDEX